CONVEYANCING

SECOND EDITION

Ross Coates MBE, LLB
Solicitor

SERIES EDITOR
CM Brand, Solicitor and Lecturer in Law
University of Liverpool

© Longman Group UK Ltd 1990

Published by

Longman Law, Tax and Finance
21/27 Lamb's Conduit Street
London WC1N 3NJ

Associated Offices:
Australia, Hong Kong, Malaysia, Singapore, USA

ISBN 0 85121 6986

A CIP catalogue record for this book is available
from the British Library

Phototypeset by Input Typesetting Ltd., London.
Printed in Great Britain by Biddles Ltd, Guildford, Surrey.

CONTENTS

CHAPTER 1

BASIC INFORMATION

1.1 Introduction

Conveyancing is a process which is implemented after the owner of a legal estate in land has decided he wishes to sell, and becomes a potential seller. On finding a willing buyer the conveyancing process will begin and the conveyancer has to start work.

1.2 The statutory sources of law

The law relating to modern conveyancing begins with the Law of Property Act in 1925. This replaced previous legislation and reduced the number of legal estates to two. The Law of Property Act 1925 contains a number of sections which are of direct practical relevance to the modern conveyancer and which are referred to in this book. It has been subsequently amended, most recently by the Law of Property (Miscellaneous Provisions) Act 1989. The year 1925 is also significant in that the concept of registered conveyancing (which had commenced during the nineteenth century) was greatly elevated in importance by the Land Registration Act 1925. There are many similarities between the conveyancing procedures involved in registered and unregistered title. By 1 December 1990, all districts in England and Wales will become compulsorily registrable and accordingly the procedure related to unregistered conveyancing will slowly decline in importance. Registered conveyancing is intended to speed the conveyancing process and to simplify it, but it can nevertheless become complex.

In essence, registered conveyancing replaces the traditional bundle of title deeds with a certificate of ownership and transactions are recorded at the appropriate Land Registry on the payment of a fee.

1.3 Practice between firms of solicitors

Conveyancing has been under the public microscope in recent years and this has led firms of solicitors to examine the methods they deploy. Local Law Societies sometimes recommend different practices in order to improve the image of their members and to speed the conveyancing process in their area.

This trend has culminated in the introduction by the Law Society of the National Conveyancing Protocol which was marketed on 21 March 1990 under the logo of 'TransAction'. The simplified procedure under the TransAction scheme is dealt with in a separate chapter in this book.

Broadly speaking the main contrast between the traditional approach to conveyancing and the approach recommended by the Council of the Law Society under the National Protocol is that in the former the buyer's solicitors do not receive a complete package of documentation at the outset and accordingly have to make their own local search and raise their own enquiries. In the latter case a total package is prepared by the seller's solicitors in advance of the commencement of the transaction and accordingly that package is available for despatch to the buyer's solicitors immediately a buyer is found. The National Protocol only applies where both sellers and buyers elect for its application to their particular transaction.

The significance of an undertaking given by a solicitor or licensed conveyancer should be noted. The breach of an undertaking by that person is a disciplinary matter by his or her professional body and this can have serious consequences. Quite often it is essential for the solicitor to provide undertakings during the course of a conveyancing transaction in order to assist the transaction to proceed speedily and smoothly to completion. An exchange of undertakings is an important feature of modern conveyancing practice. Two of the most common occasions on which they are used relate to exchange of contracts and the discharge of subsisting mortgages in favour of major banks and building societies.

1.4 The background to conveyancing

1.4.1 Legal estates Since 1 January 1926 there can be only two types of legal estate in land. These are:

- A fee simple absolute in possession which is usually referred to as a 'freehold' and an owner of this has two rights:
  (a) he enjoys ownership, and
  (b) he enjoys the benefit of occupying the land.
  He can dispose of these two rights at the same time and would do so by selling the freehold with vacant possession
- A term of years absolute which is the lesser of the two legal estates and is usually referred to as a 'leasehold'. The commencement and ending of the term must be reasonably ascertainable so that the

tenant (lessee) is not left in any doubt as to the period the lease is to run.

The tenant may assign or transfer his right of occupation for such a period as may at the time of the sale be left to run. With a business lease the landlord's consent to this may be necessary.

As an alternative to assignment the tenant, subject to the terms of the lease, may grant an underlease for a shorter period than his own lease. The tenant then becomes the immediate landlord and the original landlord becomes the head landlord. The process of granting underleases can continue for a series of shorter periods.

From the above it can be seen that in respect of one property there can be any number of legal estates. This emphasises the importance of addressing one's attention to the type of legal estate one is being instructed to buy or sell on behalf of a client.

A freeholder can sell his right of ownership having leased away his right of occupation and thereby sells the property subject to the lease. This type of freehold is called a reversion. A reversion amounts to the expectation that the right of occupation will revert back to the freeholder when the period of the lease comes to an end. This, in fact, gives the landlord the legal right to collect the rent and to enforce the other obligations in the lease. Clearly, this bold statement has been significantly modified by statute but these statutory modifications are beyond the scope of this book.

1.4.2 Legal interests The reason that land is so very different from any other property is due to the multiplicity of interests which can exist in a parcel of land and the fact that rights may be enjoyed over adjacent or nearby land. In order to enjoy one's land it may be necessary to have limited rights over the property of another and such rights are described as legal interests. Examples of legal interests are a right of way, a right of drainage or a right to draw water.

A legal interest is different from a legal estate because it includes neither a right of ownership nor a right of occupation. It must exist for a period equivalent to either a fee simple or a term of years absolute. Rights granted for a lesser term might only exist as a licence and therefore depend on the personal relationship between the grantee and the grantor for their enforcement.

A buyer for value is bound by all legal interests whether or not he has notice of them.

The holder of a legal mortgage only has a legal interest as he does not own the land or enjoy a right of occupation. The borrowers remain the owner with the normal rights of an owner throughout the duration of the mortgage.

1.4.3 Equitable interests Broadly speaking, these are interests in the land of another which are informally created or created for a period which is not equivalent to a legal estate.

The buyer for value is not bound by these interests unless he has notice of them and where appropriate they should be registered as land charges or be protected by notice or caution in the case of registered land.

1.4.4 Joint ownership of land by individuals Anyone can own a legal estate in land as long as he is aged over eighteen and is not suffering from serious disability which prevents him from dealing with his affairs.

The Law of Property Act 1925 provides that four is the maximum number of co-owners of a legal estate. It is appropriate to mention a difficult concept at this juncture. There are two facets of property, namely:

- the legal ownership
- the beneficial ownership.

Joint owners will hold the legal estate as joint tenants and will each be legally entitled to the whole unless the contrary is stated. With regard to the beneficial ownership they may be entitled to a division of the proceeds either as joint tenants or as tenants in common.

The distinction between joint tenants and tenants in common is important:

- On the death of a joint tenant the whole of his interest in the land passes to the survivor(s).
- On the death of a tenant in common his interest in the proceeds of sale does not go to the survivor but will pass under his will or intestacy as part of his estate.

Joint tenancy as to the beneficial interest is usual in personal relationships such as between husband and wife and tenancy in common is usual in business relationships such as professional partnerships. Pursuant to the above the following four conditions must be satisfied for a joint tenancy to exist:

- Each joint tenant must be entitled to possession of the whole and not part.
- Each joint tenant must have the same financial interest in the land.
- Each joint tenant must take by the same instrument.
- Each joint tenant must hold the property from and for the same time, eg fee simple absolute.

If any one of the above four items does not apply, there is a tenancy in common in relation to the proceeds of sale (the beneficial ownership).

Joint tenancy can be severed by one joint tenant serving written notice on the other or others. From service this creates a tenancy in common in respect of the proceeds of sale.

Joint tenants have a legal right under the Law of Property Act 1925 to call for the property to be sold so that each may take his specified share. The court might grant such an application where the original purpose for which the property was bought has ceased.

1.4.5   Corporate ownership   Incorporated organisations such as public and private companies own land in their own right and they can buy and sell in the same way as an individual or a group of individuals.

The contract is signed on behalf of the company by a duly authorised director or secretary and deeds are sealed with the company's own seal affixed pursuant to a resolution passed by the board of directors and attested by a director and the secretary.

1.4.6   Conveyancing on behalf of the owner   By due process of law it may be that a mortgagee exercises the power of sale conferred upon him by the Law of Property Act 1925 where the borrower defaults on his repayments.

Similarly, the owner of land may become bankrupt and the land will then vest in the trustee in bankruptcy who has a duty to sell for the benefit of the creditors. In either event the property can be sold on the appropriate evidence being adduced.

An agent may sell on behalf of an owner. In order to avoid personal liability he must act within his authority. His authority may be in writing only but before an agent signs a deed on behalf of an owner he must be appointed by a validly drawn power of attorney.

CHAPTER 2

UNREGISTERED CONVEYANCING: FREEHOLDS

2.1 Facts to be obtained from the seller

The art of conveyancing depends as much upon a methodical assembly of information as it does upon knowledge of the law. It is vital to obtain all the information required from the client at the outset to enable the proposed transaction to be efficiently set up.

Usually the proposed seller will telephone you and upon confirmation of instructions the following information should be noted:

(1) The client's full name, address and telephone number, and the address of the property being sold.
(2) The name and address of the estate agents.
(3) A description of the property being sold including its current use.
(4) The agreed sale price and a note of any additional items included in that price.
(5) Details of any conditions attaching to the sale, such as whether there is a time schedule which must be adhered to or whether there is a dependent purchase. It is important that from the outset both seller and buyer are like minded about any envisaged time schedule.
(6) The whereabouts of the title deeds. Without these it is not possible to prepare a draft contract. If the title deeds are not in the seller's possession and if there is no mortgage, they may have been deposited with the seller's bank or with another firm of solicitors. It is also important to check whether there is more than one set of title deeds. In rural situations, clients often purchase parcels of land at different intervals. Where property is in mortgage, the deeds will be deposited with that mortgagee and details of the current mortgage should additionally be obtained. The deeds will be released to a solicitor or licensed conveyancer subject to an undertaking that they will be returned to the mortgagee on demand or in lieu thereof the mortgage must be redeemed.

It is increasingly common practice for a mortgagee to allow the seller's legal representative to act for them as well. However, in certain instances a mortgagee will wish to appoint someone else and in such cases the title deeds will not be released but copies supplied instead.

(7) Details of the buyer will be ascertained from the selling agent. If there is no agent, this information must be obtained from the client seller.

2.2   Facts to be obtained from the buyer

(1) The client's name and address and telephone number.

(2) The name and address of the seller and the estate agents.

(3) Whether any preliminary deposit has been paid to the estate agents, and, if so, how much. This will need to be taken into account before exchange of contracts. Payment of a preliminary deposit is no more than a token gesture of good faith and does not constitute a legal commitment to buy.

(4) Address of the property together with a description of the property, its current and proposed use and any peculiarities such as footpaths which may go across it or tenancies to which it may be subject. The proposed buyer will have only a broad idea of such matters but such a conversation with him can alert a conveyancer to the sort of problems to be looked out for.

(5) In whose name is the property to be vested? There are many possibilities and it should be noted that four is the maximum number of people in whom the legal estate in land may be vested.

(6) The source of finance and mortgage arrangements; it is important to ensure that the proposed buyer has fully considered the financial implications of the move and, in particular, you should alert him to the expenses incurred in conveyancing such as stamp duty, agent's fees, legal fees and search fees.

Broadly speaking, application for a mortgage advance from a building society requires a written application together with a payment of a valuation fee to the society. After the property has been valued for the society and after the applicant's means have been checked, the building society will be recommended to make an offer which in some cases requires express acceptance by the applicant. Instructions will also be sent to the legal representatives.

(7) The agreed price which may be apportioned as between the legal estate and the contents of the property. Stamp duty is payable on the legal estate but not on the contents such as curtains, carpets or garden ornaments. At the time of writing the threshold of payment of stamp duty is £30,000. A transaction which is on the

threshold of £30,000 may benefit significantly from an apportionment of the price between the legal estate and the contents of the property.

(8) The proposed completion date in general terms.

2.2.1 The survey An independent survey is important to check the condition of the property because of the rule of 'caveat emptor'. This rule means that one buys the property at one's own risk save for unqualified representations made about its condition by the seller in replies to pre-contractual enquiries.

2.3   Assembly of information to prepare a draft contract

The preparation of a draft contract is the task of the seller's legal representative and is the addition of the information acquired directly from the seller or the estate agents together with the information contained in the deeds and documents of title.

The draft contract should now incorporate the new Standard Conditions of Sale (First Edition). This represents a merger of the previous Law Society and National Conditions of Sale, use of which is being discontinued. The new conditions are considerably simplified and written in plain English. The terms 'buyer' and 'seller' are used rather than purchaser and vendor. Solicitors may produce their own contract on word processors and are permitted to reproduce the standard contract incorporating the Standard Conditions of Sale by reference.

The conditions are available in a printed booklet which solicitors are advised to provide to their client in instances where the conditions are incorporated by reference. The new conditions of sale have been drafted for both domestic and commercial transactions and are not restricted to transactions where the National Protocol is followed.

2.4   Drafting the contract

The standard conditions do not need to be expressly referred to unless an alteration is sought.

The following information needs to be put on the front page:

(1) The agreement date and the name and address of the seller and the buyer. The date is left blank until contracts are actually exchanged.

(2) The description of the property together with the interest being sold by the seller. In the case of unregistered land this description

should be by reference to an attached plan. The description of the property will generally be similar to that contained in the conveyance to the seller but sometimes such descriptions need to be improved by updating. The description of the property should include easements, such as rights of way which the property enjoys, rights of light across neighbouring property or support from neighbouring property. The description will also include all exceptions and reservations in favour of the seller the benefit of which is to be sold to the buyer.

(3) If the property is sold subject to restrictive covenants contained in the title deeds, these should be noted as burdens on the property. Sometimes the root deed itself will refer to the restrictive covenants and sometimes new restrictive covenants will be imposed in this transaction, for example, if it is a sale of part only of the seller's property. In any of these events, a special condition needs to be inserted in order to make it clear which restrictions the property is being sold subject to, and copies of any restrictive covenants should be supplied. As an alternative to restrictive covenants, (eg, the buyer may build only one single storey dwelling on the land hereby agreed to be sold) there may be positive covenants which the buyer is to be required to observe (eg, the buyer must erect a larchlap fence on the length of the left hand boundary of the property). If there is a positive covenant not only should this be referred to but also the buyer should be required to enter into an indemnity covenant in the conveyance to him in respect of the future observance thereof. The reason for an indemnity is that such a covenant does not automatically pass on each transaction; the burden of it needs to be handed down expressly to each subsequent buyer.

(4) It is necessary to disclose the capacity in which the seller sells. There are a number of alternatives:

(a) Beneficial owner. This embraces the situation where a husband and wife own property as joint tenants in equity. A beneficial owner is therefore one who owns the legal estate for the benefit of himself.

(b) Mortgagee. Sometimes it may be necessary for a mortgagee, for example a bank or building society, to exercise its powers under the Law of Property Act 1925 as enhanced by the provisions of the relevant mortgage deed in order to take possession of a property from a defaulting borrower. The ultimate sanction and one which is most commonly applied is for the mortgagee to sell.

(c) Personal representatives. Where the proprietor of the legal estate has died, the sellers will be the personal representatives of his estate. When title is deduced the sellers will be obliged to produce a grant of probate or a grant of letters of administration to show they are entitled to sell. A certified copy or office copy of this must be handed over on completion.

(d) Trustees. The sellers may act as trustees for sale, and sell in that capacity. The trustees for sale would commonly include the owners of business property, and at least two individual trustees are required in order to give good receipt to a buyer of the proceeds of sale.

(e) The least common, but worthy of note is a seller acting as a tenant for life. A tenant for life will be one who is entitled to a life interest under the provisions of a settlement and even though that interest merely confers upon him an equitable interest, he has the power to sell the legal estate. Proceeds of sale must be paid to the trustees of the settlement, who again, must be at least two in number unless they are a trust corporation, (eg, a bank). Before exercising the power of sale, the trustee for life must give one month's notice to the trustees stating the price which he has accepted and that this must be the best price available. Upon receipt of the proceeds of sale the trustees must invest them for the tenant for life and his successors in title.

(5) The completion date should be inserted when contracts are exchanged, otherwise standard condition 6 will prevail.

(6) Interest payable if completion is delayed. This provision may cause confusion to clients as they will not understand that it only relates to a late completion date. The provision normally provides for the buyer to pay interest on the balance purchase money and this should now be fixed at the Law Society's Interest Rate. The rate is published regularly in the Law Society's Gazette.

(7) The root of title or title number. For unregistered conveyancing, the provisions of the Law of Property Act 1969 provide that a good root of title is a conveyance on sale or legal mortgage which is at least fifteen years old. If there is no such deed of that age, then one has to trace the title back further until a deed is found. Bad roots of title include leases (when one is conveying the freehold), wills and equitable mortgages. In certain transactions one might be requested to accept a root of title which is less than fifteen years old or a document other than a mortgage, or a conveyance on sale as the root deed. On these occasions further enquiries should be made in order to ascertain why the request is being put. It may mean that the legal title to the property is defective, and if this is so, certain remedial steps may be necessary such as obtaining a defective title indemnity policy from an insurance company and a statutory declaration from the seller or

his neighbours. Such additional requirements may give rise to a special condition being attached to the back of the contract.

(8) The price of the property being sold and provision for a deposit. Sometimes these are left blank until exchange of contracts is imminent. It saves having to re-type the contract if the transaction does not proceed and the contract is required for an alternative proposed buyer. Where a deposit is inserted the standard conditions provide for this to be 10% of the price. However, a deposit of less than 10% may sometimes be agreed by negotiation between the parties' legal representatives, and this negotiation usually takes place immediately before contracts are exchanged. It may necessitate a further special condition on the back of the contract.

The deposit does constitute clients' money and the seller is entitled to interest earned on the deposit money in accordance with the provisions of the Financial Services Act 1986.

The standard conditions provide that if the seller is buying another property in a related transaction, he may use all or part of the deposit as a deposit in that transaction, to be held in that transaction as stakeholder. This means it may not be further used. Any part of a deposit which is not required as described above, must be held as stakeholder by the seller's solicitor until completion. If this arrangement is to be varied a special condition is required.

(9) Sometimes the amount payable for chattels at the property may be separately set out, particularly if the price of the property is close to the current stamp duty threshold.

2.4.1   Special conditions   These are included for the purpose of supplementing the standard conditions of sale, and for the purpose of altering the standard conditions of sale. It is not possible to provide the reader with a comprehensive list of these, because they vary from one transaction to another. The pre-printed special conditions are self evident from the copy of the form set out in Chapter 8. The following are examples of additional special conditions:–

(1) Whether the sale is with vacant possession on completion, or subject to an existing tenancy. In the latter case, details should be inserted.

(2) The authorised use of the property for the purposes of current planning legislation.

(3) An attempt to avoid liability on the part of the seller for any representations given by him or on his behalf save for replies to enquiries given by the seller's solicitor and stating that the buyer proceeds entirely on the basis of his own survey and inspection.

2.5 Preliminary enquiries

Upon receipt of the draft contract in duplicate together with the accompanying plan and any copy covenants, the buyer's solicitor will turn his attention to making an index map search and a local search and also to raising enquiries before contract. Enquiries before contract are a method of ascertaining as much practical information as possible from the seller about the property to be bought. The buyer's solicitor will generally send a standard form to the seller's solicitor accompanied by a copy and also further questions which ideally should be tailor-made for the particular transaction. A standard form of enquiries is contained in Chapter 8.

Questions which are commonly asked are as follows:

(1) The ownership and maintenance responsibilities of the boundaries of the property. Ownership of boundaries is commonly marked on deed plans with an inwardly facing 'T'. There will be occasions where there is no indication with the title deeds as to who owns the boundaries and in that case custom and practice will prevail.

(2) Disputes. The seller will be required to supply information about any disputes he has had with the neighbours in the recent past.

(3) Notices. The seller will be expected to supply details of any correspondence he may have had with the local authority in respect of planning matters either relating to the property to be sold or to neighbouring property. Sometimes an older property will have been listed as a building of special architectural or historical interest and again details should be supplied. A notice may have been served with regard to an intention by a local authority compulsorily to purchase the property or part of it and again notices may have been received by the seller where the property is subject to occupation by a tenant.

(4) Guarantees. The property may be sold with the benefit of certain guarantees to its conditions. The most common of these is the Buildmark guarantee supplied by the National House Building Council. Details of this appear below.

Other guarantees may be supplied by a double glazing company or a damp-proofing company or a woodworm treatment company. Details of all these should be supplied to the buyer's solicitor on request.

(5) Services. The buyer will wish to know which services he has the benefit of and here we refer to gas and mains water. It may well be that the property does not have the benefit of main drainage and this will lead to the further enquiry as to arrangements for

septic tank drainage, whether or not that septic tank drains onto neighbouring property and, if so, what rights are in existence for such an arrangement. Similarly, the buyer will wish to know whether there are rights for services to pass over neighbouring land.

(6) Exclusive facilities. This deals with those facilities enjoyed exclusively by the property to be sold over neighbouring property. Most commonly, this might relate to a right of way across the neighbouring property, and details as to whether or not that right has been interrupted or whether charges have been made for its use will be required.

(7) Shared facilities. This enquiry is similar to the one above but refers to those facilities which are jointly used by neighbours over a third person's property. Again, details of maintenance responsibilities will be required and the proportion in which the costs of upkeep have been shared by those entitled.

(8) This enquiry refers to the rights of those who do not actually own the property but who may, for example, occupy it. Adult occupiers should be required to sign the contract on completion in order to signify their consent to granting vacant possession in accordance with the obligations of the owners on exchange of contracts. Details of occupiers including their names and ages will be required in answer to preliminary enquiries.

(9) Restrictions. It will be necessary to confirm that all restrictions have been observed and if they have not been observed to confirm that consent to vary or discharge them has been forthcoming. A restrictive covenant imposed after 1925 binds future owners if registered as a land charge class D(ii) or on the land register. Earlier covenants affect buyer's for value if they buy with notice.

(10) It is necessary to state current use of the property and whether that has been continuous. Where a property is being used in breach of planning permission, an enforcement notice may be served by the local planning authority on the owner/occupier requiring the use to cease. Failure to observe that enforcement notice can result in a prosecution in the local magistrates' court. The existence or otherwise of an enforcement notice will be revealed by the local search result. Once an enforcement notice has been entered against a property as a local land charge it will not be removed. This will not materially affect the buyer unless he is seeking to continue with the unauthorised use.

(11) It is increasingly common practice amongst solicitors to supply a list for completion by the seller in order to answer the question about fixtures and fittings.

(12) Unless a completion date is expressly agreed it will be fixed by the general conditions of sale.

Preliminary enquiries should be treated seriously and the seller's legal representative should do his best to supply full answers. The treatment of preliminary enquiries has been recently commented on by the Conveyancing Standards Committee of the Law Society and their recommendations are set out in *Preliminary Enquiries: House Purchase, A Practice Recommendation* (Longman 1987).

2.6 Quality of the building

Pursuant to the Defective Premises Act 1972 a developer is required to build dwellings properly in a workmanlike manner. This does provide protection to buyers except where the builder goes bankrupt or disappears.

2.6.1 The National House Building Council This was set up in order to provide the buyers of a new property with a nationally underwritten scheme to enable them to feel satisfied with the condition of their property at the time of completion of the building. The scheme was divided into two parts. First, full cover is provided for two years against a wide variety of defects. The procedure is that if any such defects arise, then the aggrieved buyer should first make a complaint to the builder in the hope that the builder will then voluntarily put matters right. Should he fail to do so or should he have gone out of business, then the matter will be taken up formally by the NHBC who will pay compensation in an appropriate case.

The remaining eight years of the ten-year period are covered by a basic insurance against major structural defects.

The structure of the scheme has recently been changed so that it is now described as the 'Buildmark Scheme', the operation of which is described below.

The benefit of the NHBC guarantee can be assigned to a buyer who buys a propery within ten years of the date of its construction. It is not essential that there is a formal assignment of the benefit of cover. The first buyer is issued with an 'offer of cover' which he must accept by completing and signing the acceptance form. This is returned to the NHBC at Chiltern Avenue, Amersham, Bucks who issue a 'ten-year notice' when the home has been completed. The buyer should keep these forms in the Buildmark booklet.

2.6.2 Surveys The fundamental importance of a legal representative advising his client to have a formal survey prior to exchange of contracts has already been made. The seller's solicitor is very careful about answering any questions relating to the condition of the property and will generally qualify all the seller's comments about the structural condition of the property by stating that no warranty is given.

There are three categories of inspection that the property may receive. A mortgagee may only be concerned with a valuation of the property and such valuations cannot be regarded as surveys. Better than a valuation but not so thorough as a structural survey is a 'home buyer's report'. A home buyer's report represents a special form of survey which is not fully comprehensive but does deal with the most important aspects of the property's condition. It is less expensive than a structural survey and the terms of the report will be presented on a standard format containing a number of exclusion clauses.

A structural survey is the most comprehensive inspection of a property which is possible.

Should the buyer have any complaints about the condition of the property after he has completed his purchase, then in the above cases it will be the surveyor rather than the seller to whom he should apply.

2.6.3   Architect's certificates   These are issued to a builder at the completion of appropriate stages of building for the purpose of releasing stage payments from a purchaser and for a small builder may replace the role of the NHBC.

2.7   Searches

2.7.1   Local land charges search   The first search commonly undertaken at the outset of a transaction is a local search. There are two parts to this. Firstly, there is form LLC1 which is submitted in duplicate. This form reveals the existence or otherwise of any local land charges (see Chapter 8).

When the form is completed it should either be despatched to the appropriate London borough council or outside London to the appropriate district council. They administer these searches although they do not necessarily supply all the information themselves. The form should be addressed to the Registrar of Local Land Charges.

The result of this part of the search will reveal such matters as:

- Enforcement notices
- Whether the property is subject to outstanding conditions in respect of an improvement grant. These conditions generally prevail for a period of five years from the date that the improvement

grant is registered and may, *inter alia*, prevent the seller selling to a non-owner/occupier.

- Sometimes planning permission is subject to the provisions of what is commonly known as a 'section 52 agreement'. A s 52 agreement (Town and Country Planning Act 1971) is an agreement negotiated between the local authority and the developer and permits the building works subject to the observation of a number of mutually agreed factors. This agreement is commonly registered as a local land charge and expressly draws the buyer's attentions to its provisions. See C M Brand and D W Williams, *Planning Law for Conveyancers*, 3rd ed (Longman, 1989). The above are a selection of examples.

The second part of the enquiries addressed to the local authority comprises a list of questions asked on form Con29A except in London where the form used is form Con29D (see Chapter 8).

The appropriate form is sent in duplicate to the district council or London borough with the local land charges search referred to above. The current fee for dealing with both is £26 unless Part II and further additional enquiries are raised in which case extra fees will be payable. Forms Con29A and Con29D are divided into two parts. The first part deals with standard enquiries which relate to all properties. The second part comprises a number of additional enquiries which of their very nature will only relate to certain properties in certain locations, eg does a public path traverse the property?

A comprehensive guide to the contents of forms Con29A and Con29D is to be found in Trevor Aldridge, *Guide to Enquiries of Local Authorities* (Longman, 1982). Perhaps the most practically significant questions asked are as follows:

- Does the property abut a publicly maintained highway? If it does not, express rights of way are required, and the contents of the draft contract will need to be checked for rights of way. Such rights of way will normally be accompanied by maintenance obligations.

  Where a new property has been constructed on a development, the new road may not have been adopted at the date of undertaking the local search. In the absence of formal adoption by the relevant highway authority, one would expect to find what is commonly known as a 'section 38 agreement'. This agreement is made pursuant to s 38 of the Highways Act 1980 and normally requires a new road to be made up to a specified standard and maintained for a year. The agreement may join in a bank or similar institution as guarantor. The developer will be required to make up the road to the necessary standard and assuming all goes well, the road will be adopted without cost to the frontages.

- Enquiry 5 will indicate whether or not the property has the benefit of mains drainage. An isolated rural property will probably have its own private drainage system. A new property on a development will eventually expect to drain into the mains drainage system and here care is required. The adoption of the mains drains generally follows the adoption of the highway but arrangements are different. Under the Public Health Act 1936, s 18 the water authority can agree to adopt a private sewer or drain. The conveyancer must check the precise arrangements.
- There are a number of questions relating to planning matters. Question 7 deals with the existence or otherwise of a structure plan for the area. It is important to make it clear to one's client whether or not such a structure plan has been inspected as this might affect the possibility of new buildings in the vicinity of the property or the alteration of existing arrangements of terms of use.

It is generally agreed that local authority search results last for two months. However, under TransAction, a search up to six months old may be validated under an insurance indemnity scheme. (See below.) Forms Con29A and Con29D are available in a short form as well as in their long form. Most authorities accept the short forms but some do not.

2.7.2 Commons registration search   Such a search is important when dealing with conveyancing of vacant land. The search is made on form CR21 which is despatched to the relevant county council together with a fee of £6.00 and a plan. The point of such a search is that land to be the subject of the transaction may be registered by the local authority as having rights of common registered over it in favour of owners and occupiers of other properties in the vicinity pursuant to the Commons Registration Act 1965. There will be a register of those entitled together with the purposes of which they are entitled.

2.7.3 Index map search   An index map search is important on the occasion of conveying unregistered land. The search should be made on the appropriate form and is addressed to the District Land Registry for the area in which the property is located. The prescribed form requires the insertion of the address of the property and preferably should be accompanied by a suitable plan. The search costs £6 and the result generally follows quickly. The result indicates whether or not the property has already been registered and, if so, with what title number. If it has not been registered, it indicates whether there are any adverse matters which will have to be noted on the register on the occasion of first registration.

2.7.4 Land charges department search A search in the Land Charges Department which is based at Plymouth should be done both before exchange of contracts and before completion in order to protect the inerests of the prospective buyer. The search is relevant to unregistered land only and should be carried out on the prescribed form K15. The form is completed as follows:

- Insert the full name of the seller of the property.
- Insert the period of years to be searched. The period of years should coincide with the seller's ownership of the property.
- Insert the county, and former county if appropriate, where the property is situated.
- It is not essential to insert the address of the property although there is provision for this.

Each name costs £1 to search and the total is paid by inserting the firm's credit account number on the bottom of the form adjacent to the firm's name and address.

It is important to have a series of search results in respect of all estate owners of the property since 1925. Although one only has to see title for a minimum period of fifteen years, any registrations against earlier estate owners such as those relating to restrictive covenants constitute actual notice to subsequent buyers and accordingly a clear series of land charges searches are necessary.

If the buyer is raising mortgage finance, it will be important to undertake a bankruptcy search against his name before completion. A bankruptcy search is undertaken on form K16 and on that form it is only necessary to state the names to be searched.

It is to be hoped that the land charges search result will reveal 'no subsisting entries'. Where this is not the case the following are the more common entries:

- Pending actions relate to subsisting court actions which remain unresolved and which relate to an interest in the land. These are revealed as 'PA'.
- Writs or orders affecting the land such as a charging order entered pursuant to a judgment of the court. These are referred to as 'WO'.
- Class C(i) is a legal mortgage not protected by the deposit of the deeds and documents. This is commonly known as a 'puisne mortgage' and relates to a second or subsequent mortgage.
- Class C(iv) is a contract by someone who is entitled to have a legal estate conveyed to him including a valid option of purchase or a

right of pre-emption ('an estate contract'). This is often used where there is a protracted period between exchange of contracts and completion and the proposed buyer wishes to ensure that the vendor does not deal elsewhere in the intervening months.

- Class D(ii) is a restrictive covenant created after 1925.
- Class D(iii) is an equitable easement created after 1925. It relates, for example, to a benefit over neighbouring land which has been informally granted.
- Class F is the right of a spouse (commonly the wife) to occupy the matrimonial home though having no legal estate therein under the Matrimonial Homes Act 1967, as amended.

The search result is codified as above together with the date of the registration and the number of the registration. Should further details be required, it is possible to make application to the Land Charges Department for an office copy. There is a fee payable of £1.00 for each office copy.

Sometimes the entries revealed will either not relate to the property in question or to the individual seller. In these circumstances the buyer's legal representative will ask the seller's legal representative to certify the search result in order to confirm that the entry does not relate to the subject matter of the current transaction.

Searches on the above may be undertaken by telephone or by teleprinter and in either case the cost increases by £2.00 per name.

It is also possible to apply by facsimile transmission and the Land Charges Department have lines open to receive such transmissions during normal business hours between Monday and Friday (Fax No. Plymouth (0752) 766666 – 5 lines). Where possible applications should be made by post unless application is urgent. The fax facility is only open to credit account holders and is available to receive applications only. The results will be posted.

2.7.5 Company search The Companies Registration Office in Cardiff maintains up-to-date information from those companies who have supplied necessary information via their annual return or otherwise. Such information may not be disclosed by the result of a land charges search. The search result will reveal whether or not the company is in receivership or in liquidation and also, and more commonly, whether or not there are fixed or floating charges. Fixed charges should be redeemed before completion. If the company is a developer, it is likely that a deed of release will be handed over in respect of a particular property being sold so that the mortgage attaches instead to the retained properties. If there are only floating charges, these will not need to be redeemed but it will be necessary to ensure they have not 'crystallised'. A letter from the chargee will suffice.

A company search is done before completion where the seller is a company.

2.7.6. Coal mining searches Such a search is important in those counties where coal mining either does or used to take place. Such properties may be subject to possible subsidence. The standard form of enquiry agreed by British Coal and the Law Society should be used. Supplies of the forms and of a directory which identifies those counties in which a search is appropriate is available from Law Stationers.

The fee required for such a search is £16.85 in respect of each standard form of enquiry submitted to British Coal. No coal mining enquiry would be required in respect of property in Bedfordshire, Buckinghamshire, Cambridgeshire, Cornwall, Devon, Dorset, East Sussex, Essex, Greater London, Hampshire, Hertfordshire, Norfolk, Suffolk, Surrey, West Sussex and Wiltshire. The standard form is intended for use in connection with domestic property and the enquiries relate to:

- Past underground coal mining.
- Present underground coal mining.
- Future underground coal mining.
- Shafts and adits.
- Surface geology.
- Claims for subsidence damage.
- Open cast for coal mining.

The standard form should be used in conjunction with a further form when dealing with non-domestic property.

2.8 Mortgage finance

2.8.1 Sources of mortgage finance These are banks, building societies, insurance offices and a growing number of mortgage companies. The formalities they will adopt vary but it is the duty of the buyer's solicitor to ensure that contracts are not exchanged until after the mortgage offer has been received and solicitors have been instructed.

The maximum amount available to a buyer will depend upon both his income and the value of the property. Institutions will generally provide a mortgage advance of between two and three times the income of the borrower but this might depend on the prevailing interest rate and the borrower's other commitments.

Where a high percentage loan is made against the property, a mortgage guarantee policy may be required in respect of which the single premium will commonly be deducted from the mortgage advance on completion. It is vital to read mortgage instructions carefully to see whether the lending institution proposes to make any deductions from the mortgage advance and to discuss this with the borrower carefully. Sometimes conditions attaching to an offer impose a penalty for early redemption. This should be drawn to the buyer's attention.

2.8.2 Acting both for buyer and mortgagee   The interests of both are similar. They are both concerned to ensure they obtain a good title to the property. Searches are done for the benefit of both parties save as mentioned above.

One must ensure that the mortgage deed is completed properly and duly executed prior to the completion day. The borrower should understand the nature of mortgage lending and should recognise the meaning of some of the more important conditions attached to the mortgage advance. Generally speaking, mortgage deeds are very briefly drawn and there is a conditions booklet setting out conditions incorporated by reference.

The Law of Property Act 1925 confers important powers on mortgagees where there is default. Sometimes these powers are improved and enhanced by the provisions of a mortgage deed.

Other conditions attaching to a mortgage offer generally relate to the condition of the property requiring an undertaking by a borrower to do certain work within a certain period of time after completion. Sometimes a retention is made from the mortgage advance until stipulated works are finished. If the road in front of the property is not adopted at the time of completion, it is common for a small sum to be held back until either the production of a s 38 agreement or the road is formally adopted, and which is required will be clear from the mortgage conditions.

If the mortgage is an endowment mortgage, there will be one or more endowment policies which will either have to be assigned in favour of the mortgagee or deposited with the title deeds upon completion. Again, it is the duty of the borrower's legal representative to check that such policies have been issued. Notice of deposit or assignment must be given to the insurance company after completion of the mortgage.

2.8.3 Types of mortgages   In an ordinary repayment scheme the mortgage advance is repayable in full over the prescribed period which is most commonly twenty or twenty-five years and both interest and principal are repaid to the institution concerned. Initially, the major part of the repayment is interest and it is not until the later years that the capital is reduced significantly.

In an *endowment mortgage scheme* the mortgage advance is coupled with an endowment policy to the full amount of the sum borrowed. On the basis that the policy is in existence, one merely repays interest to the institution lending the money at the same time as the premiums under a given policy. After the expiry of the given period, the sum of money which has accrued under the endowment policy will at least be sufficient to repay the principal to the lending institution and there should be an excess for the borrower. The overall cost of an endowment mortgage may be very similar to that of a repayment mortgage.

Sometimes a repayment mortgage can be coupled with a *mortgage protection policy*. In such a case a small monthly premium is paid to an insurance company so that if the borrower dies before the end of the period of the mortgage, the amount borrowed is then paid off. This is automatically built into the endowment mortgage system.

2.8.4 Common provisions

- If the borrower wishes to create a lease, he must consult his mortgagee and seek his permission.
- The most common system of enforcing rights against a defaulting borrower is the power of sale. The power is implied by virtue of ss 101–103 of the Law of Property Act 1925 and may additionally be expressly stated in the mortgage deed. The power arises as soon as the legal date for redemption has passed which will be after the first few months of the mortgage advance. The power must have become exercisable which will occur as follows:

    (a) when the interest is two months in arrears;

    (b) when there is a breach of a covenant in the mortgage deed other than the covenant to repay;

    (c) when there is failure to repay the loan, although three months' notice has been given.

    A mortgagor cannot prevent the sale after a contract has been exchanged. The mortgagee must act in good faith to obtain a property price and apply the proceeds of sale in the prescribed way; any surplus must be held in trust for the mortgagor. Where a borrower is in difficulties, the major lenders may opt to lengthen the term rather than enforce their rights of sale.

- It is also possible for the mortgagor to appoint a receiver and to foreclose but these powers are rarely exercised.
- The first mortgagee is protected by the deposit of the title deeds and this is sufficient to prevent dealings with the land without his consent. Second and subsequent mortgages are protected by the registration of a puisne mortgage on form K1 at the Land Charges Department.

2.8.5   The MIRAS scheme

Mortgage interest relief at source allows certain borrowers to deduct basic rate income tax from their interest payments. These arrangements are contained in Finance Act 1982, ss 26–29 and apply to payments of relevant loan interest by a qualifying borrower to a qualifying lender made on or after 1 April 1983.

Relevant loan interest is interest on a loan for the purchase of the main residence of the borrower. A qualifying borrower is any individual except one who (or whose spouse) is exempt or immune from tax under Schedule E, Case I, II or III.

Qualifying lenders include building societies, local authorities, authorised insurance companies, trustee savings banks, new town development corporations, major clearing banks and some finance houses. Qualifying borrowers deduct tax at the basic rate from relevant loan interest. Lenders are required to accept the deduction and recover tax deducted from the Revenue. Basic rate tax relief is given through MIRAS and higher rates of relief can be claimed from the Revenue.

Mortgage interest relief is given only to the extent that the amount on which interest is payable does not equal or exceed the qualifying maximum for the year of assessment. This has been set at £30,000 for a number of years. Qualifying loans in excess of the tax relief limit were included within MIRAS with effect from 6 April 1987 (Finance Act 1985, s 37).

Borrowers are able to certify to lenders that loans are for a particular qualifying purpose enabling lenders to bring such loans into MIRAS for commencement.

Loans for home improvements do not now qualify. Those with 'old loans' for this purpose should not remortgage their homes as this will lead to a loss of their tax relief through MIRAS.

2.9   Exchanging contracts

2.9.1   Acting for the buyer—when and how?   When satisfactory search results have been received and satisfactory replies have been

received to preliminary enquiries together with answers to any follow-up questions, the buyer's legal representative is in a position to approve the draft contract and to return one part to the seller's solicitor. At this stage details of the price and the name and address of the buyer will be inserted and the contract can be sent to both parties for signature. Each party's legal representative will then hold an undated but signed contract and this will be held in readiness for exchange which can be effected in a number of different ways.

If there is no related sale the buyer's solicitor can post the contract together with the agreed deposit money drawn on the solicitor's client account and made payable to the seller's legal representative. Where effecting exchange of contracts through the post, exchange occurs when the seller's solicitor posts their part back to the buyer's solicitor. From that moment on there is a binding exchange of contracts and the risk passes to the buyer who must insure the property against fire and similar perils. Where there is a related sale it is more likely that contracts will be exchanged over the telephone in accordance with the Law Society's Formulae A, B or C.

2.9.2 Acting for the seller—when and how? When acting for the seller the chief concern is to obtain the proceeds of sale and to release the seller from any obligations he may have according to the title deeds. The contract should be sent to the seller for signature.

If there is a related purchase, the contracts may be exchanged over the telephone, and the solicitors should agree a tentative date for completion with both parties and check that both parties are ready. Where one legal representative holds both contracts, Law Society Formula A is appropriate. Once ready to exchange, the legal representative holding both parts agrees that he holds his client's part to the other's order from the time that exchange takes place, and that time is duly noted. They also agree that both contract forms are dated with the date of exchange and the date for completion and the representative holding the contracts undertakes to post the client's part by first class post to the other party that same day. Contracts are then exchanged from that moment.

Under Law Society Formula B both representatives hold their clients' signed part and, where appropriate, a cheque for the agreed deposit. Again they speak on the telephone and agree to exchange with effect from a time which they both note. They both undertake to hold their client's part to the other's order and to post it by first class post that same day to the other and where appropriate this is accompanied with the deposit cheque. Contracts are then exchanged from that moment. In either event it is common to synchronise exchange by one legal representative at the beginning of a chain of transactions to say on the telephone that he 'releases' his client's part to the other so that he commits himself to exchanging contracts and provides the other representative with the freedom to enter into a binding contract within a specified period of time. The system works well in practice as many practitioners have found it impossible simultaneously to exchange contracts on the telephone thereby leaving a theoretical opportunity for one party to change his mind in the few minutes it takes to ring him back.

Under Law Society Formula C a chain of transactions may be exchanged over the telephone more satisfactorily. The solicitor at the end of the chain is asked to release his contract, for a specified period of time to the solicitor acting for the buyer next in line. Precise details of times etc should be carefully recorded and each solicitor should be available to speak to the other throughout the agreed duration of the release. Memoranda should be prepared accordingly. The solicitor in whose favour the contract has been released is then free to undertake a telephone exchange of contracts in accordance with the Law Society Formula A or B as appropriate and can then return to the original solicitor at the end of the chain in order to complete the exchange of the released contract in the same way as he would if dealing with Law Society Formula A or B. Law Society Formula C therefore involves two phone calls, but there is an obligation to proceed by the solicitor who agrees to release his contract from the moment he enters into that agreement.

It is possible to achieve simultaneous exchange of contracts with sales and purchases through the post but this takes a number of days. It is rarely used but would proceed as follows:

- The first buyer sends his contract and deposit cheque to the first seller.
- The first seller (who is also the second buyer) sends his contract and deposit cheque to the second seller.
- The second seller then completes exchange of contracts by posting his part to the second buyer and the second buyer (who is also the first seller) completes exchange by posting his contract to the first buyer.

This system works because the exchange of contracts takes place through the post when the seller posts his part and not before. There can be extremely serious consequences for failing to synchronise an exchange of contracts and it would be negligent conduct if one's client were to end up without a property at all or alternatively with two properties. For this reason some firms insist on either senior or experienced personnel dealing with the act of exchange.

After contracts are exchanged a completion date should be entered in one's diary as should the date for making the necessary land charges search in order to ensure the completion date falls within the priority period of twenty-one days.

It is also important to obtain a redemption statement from the existing building society where acting for the seller and similarly to request the estate agent's account which is customarily settled by the legal representative out of the proceeds of sale on completion. It is important to inform one's client that exchange of contracts has taken place and this can be done on the telephone followed by a letter. It is good practice to discuss the following matters with the client:

- Assistance with regard to the apportionment of rates or otherwise ensure that these are discharged up to the completion date.
- Discuss moving arrangements and check the likely whereabouts of the key on completion day.
- Ensure client has the utility meters read on completion.

Where acting for a buyer it is important to make arrangements to obtain the mortgage advance by completing the report on title for the mortgagee and despatching it to them as quickly as possible. Prepare the mortgage deeds and arrange for these to be signed by the client.

2.10   Deducing title

Even with an unregistered property it is becoming increasingly common for the legal title to be deduced before contracts are exchanged and, indeed, is the system under TranAction. The customary practice was that title was not deduced until after contracts were exchanged unless there was some defect with the title in respect of which it was desired to give express notice to the buyer's legal representative.

Once contracts are exchanged all deeds and documents of title since the root deed are assembled and photocopied. These copy deeds and documents are then pinned together attached to a prescribed list called an 'epitome of title' where contents are set out in chronological order with a note of the nature of the document, the parties to it, whether or not it is a copy, which number in the list it bears and whether the original will be handed over on completion. On receipt of the epitome the buyer's legal representative will examine the title and search carefully to check there are no defects. If he finds defects he will ask the seller's legal representative to explain them and he does this by 'raising requisitions'.

Occasionally the seller's legal representative will either send or prepare an abstract of title. The art of preparing these has now largely died out but in former times these were used as an alternative to photocopies and comprised short summaries of the deeds and documents of title prepared in accordance with recognised convention on large sheets of paper in a number of columns.

There may be more than one epitome of title as, for example, where title needs to be shown to easements which are enjoyed over neighbouring land.

The following points should be noted:

- If a buyer has married since the date of the purchase thereby changing her name a certified copy of her marriage certificate should be included with the property's title deeds.
- Where one of two joint tenants has died since the date of purchase a certified copy of the death certificate should appear with his title deeds.
- Where one of two tenants in common has died since the date of purchase it may be necessary for the surviving tenant in common to appoint a new trustee for the purposes of the conveyance to give good receipt for the purchase money.
- Where a deed is executed by an agent the buyer's representative should ask to see the original or a certified copy of the power of attorney.
- Where a tenant in common or the surviving owner or the sole owner of property dies, a certified copy of the grant of probate or grant of letters of administration should be supplied in order to verify the appointment of the personal representatives who are now to make good title.

2.11   Raising requisitions on title

The standard form of these appears in Chapter 8. Additional questions may be asked but they must relate to the title and must not duplicate previous questions. The standard form includes answers to the following:

(1) Confirmation that replies to preliminary enquiries remain unchanged.

(2) Confirmation that outgoings will be paid until the completion date and receipts will be produced. A supply of a completion statement indicating the balance required to complete.

(3) A list of the deeds and documents to be handed over on completion together with a further note of any deeds which may not be handed over and the reason why.

(4) This requires any outstanding borrowing to be discharged on or before completion and if it is not discharged before completion, an undertaking is then requested to discharge the borrowing on the completion and to remit the receipted mortgage deed to the buyer's solicitor as soon as possible. The type of suitable undertaking has been recommended by the Law Society but a majority of practitioners are content to accept an undertaking given in answers to requisitions which merely undertakes to repay the mortgage on completion and then to remit the receipted mortgage deed as soon as it is returned to them by the mortgagee in question.

(5) Confirmation that vacant possession will be given on completion and an enquiry as to the arrangements for handing over keys.

(6) This question enquires as to whether there is any third party that notice of the transaction should be delivered to. By and large this relates to the sale of leases.

(7) This question deals with the arrangements for completion such as where completion will take place and can either be physically in the seller's solicitor's office or, where a separate firm is acting for a mortgagee, in their office or more commonly today through the post. Similarly, details of the seller's solicitor's bank account are requested and thirdly an enquiry for what amount the seller's legal representative's banker's draft is required. As between solicitors operating within a given area, client account cheques may be accepted on completion but this practice depends upon local convention.

Additional requisitions relate to defects in title and the most common of these are as follows:

- Missing deeds breaking the chain of title.
- Missing land charges searches which have to be redone.
- Entries on land charge search results which have not been explained.
- Unstamped or improperly stamped deeds.
- Improperly signed deeds.
- Deeds which refer to plans which are not there, plans which are not coloured or plans which are wrongly coloured.
- A misdescription of the property or the covenants and easements which go with it.
- Old mortgages in respect of which there is no evidence of discharge.

There are additional possibilities but the above are the most common defects which might usefully be borne in mind when investigating a title.

2.12   Drafting a conveyance deed

With effect from 1st December 1990 all land in England and Wales will be subject to compulsory first registration if it is not already registered at the time of the transaction. The Land Registration rules provide that in such a case, a conveyance deed may be replaced by a transfer deed. In most transactions, the preparation of a transfer deed is more simple, as one of the prescribed forms can be used. Further detail is contained later in the text.

2.13   Making arrangements for completion

On completion the seller's legal representative should have in his possession a signed conveyance or transfer, the deeds and documents of title, knowledge of the whereabouts of the key to the property and a redemption statement in respect of any subsisting mortgage to be discharged. Generally, he will take the initiative and contact the buyer's solicitor to ascertain the arrangements preferred for the actual completion. If the completion is to be in his office, he will collect the banker's draft or solicitor's client cheque and in return hand over the bundle of deeds together with the conveyance to the buyer. Immediately thereafter he will discharge the mortgage and disburse the balance purchase money.

The buyer's solicitor will have previously ensured that he is in possession of the mortgage advance cheque on the date it is required and will then proceed to attend the seller's solicitor's office or more commonly will organise a telegraphic transfer to the seller's solicitor's bank account of the balance required. The deeds and documents of title will then be posted off by the seller's solicitor together with the conveyance to the buyer.

It is important that the buyer's solicitor is in possession of clear land charge search results to cover the date of completion and where the seller is a company he should have a clear company search against the seller.

When the buyer's solicitor is in receipt of the deeds and documents of title he should check that the originals accord with the photocopies that he was previously sent. He should also check replies to requisitions in order to ensure all additional matters have been cleared up.

If separate solicitors are representing the seller's mortgagee, completion should take place at their office instead of the seller's solicitor's office. Arrangements vary and are generally more relaxed than they once were but in such a situation careful arrangements should be made before the completion day itself.

2.13.1 Completion statements In addition to the completion statement which the seller's representative supplies to the buyer's legal representative, it is also vital that each representative provides a statement to his own client for checking. A precedent statement appears in Chapter 8 and the client should be requested to confirm his acceptance. The accompanying letter should seek consent of the client to pay estate agent's and legal fees.

2.14 Post-completion formalities

2.14.1 The seller's legal representative The seller's legal representatives will send the receipted legal charge to the buyer's legal representative as soon as it is returned from the mortgagee duly receipted. The mortgagee will generally leave the date of receipting blank and this should be inserted to coincide with the completion day.

The seller's legal representative will generally pay the estate agents and in so doing ensure that account has been taken of any preliminary deposit paid to them by the buyer. Where the mortgage which has been redeemed was an endowment mortgage the seller's legal representative will make certain that there is a deed of reassignment in respect of the endowment policy and notice of reassignment will be sent to the insurance company.

2.14.2 The buyer's legal representative The buyer's legal representative will give notice of completion to the mortgagee if this is part of the particular mortgagee's procedural requirements.

Having checked the title deeds against the copies these will be held pending the stamping of the conveyance. The conveyance deed will be sent to the appropriate office of the Inland Revenue together with the form Stamps L(A)451. A specimen of this is contained in Chapter 8. This form supplies details of the transaction together with the value of the transaction so that the amount of duty payable can be calculated. The current duties are set out in the current edition of *Conveyancing Fees and Charges*, 13th ed (Longman, 1990).

Where stamp duty is payable a cheque should be made in favour of the Inland Revenue and should accompany the conveyance, the stamps form and a schedule which are then despatched together with an additional plan of the property in appropriate cases.

Where there is a conveyance for value or an assignment for value of a leasehold with not less than forty years to run, and the property comes within an area of compulsory registration under the Land Registration Acts 1925–1988, the buyer's legal representative must apply for first registration within two months of the date of completion. This they will do by utilising land registration form 2B. It is important to submit the application for land registration before the expiry of the protection afforded by the land charges search result. The search should be renewed if this proves impossible.

CHAPTER 3

UNREGISTERED CONVEYANCING: LEASEHOLDS

3.1 Facts to be obtained from the seller

Buying and selling leasehold property follow the same principles as enunciated in Chapter 2 but are slightly more involved. The facts to be obtained from the seller are the same as those previously set out but the buyer's solicitor must also ascertain whether this is the grant of a new lease so that the seller is the freeholder or whether the seller is a leaseholder granting a sublease.

If a new lease or sublease is to be granted, it is important to ascertain the following:

- The term of years agreed.
- The rent, how it is to be paid and whether there is to be provision for reviews. The landlord may charge VAT on the rent for commercial premises. His intentions should be clarified.
- Who is to be responsible for the maintenance of the property and if the obligation is to be split between landlord and tenant, how is it to be split? This may be affected by statute.
- Who is to be responsible for paying the outgoings related to the property including the responsibility for insurance?
- Is the proposed lease to relate to residential premises, business premises or an agricultural holding? It is essential to establish which of these three applies because the law relating to each is fundamentally different and the style of preparing the lease is different. Most large firms of lawyers possess precedent forms which can be used. If it is practical, it is often sensible to visit the premises in respect of which the lease is to be granted. This helps one to establish the rights that are required for the passage of services and mutual rights of support maintenance and rights of way.

If the seller instructs you to sell an existing lease this will be described as an 'assignment' and the assignment of an existing lease obviates the need to deal with the above matters since they will have already been settled when the lease was originally granted by the landlord. If you are instructed to deal with the assignment of an existing lease, it is important to ascertain whether a premium is to be asked from the proposed assignee (VAT may be added on business premises) and to establish from the terms of the lease whether the landlord's consent will be required. Generally this is only required in respect of assignments of leases relating to business premises.

3.2   Facts to be obtained from the buyer

The buyer will either be a new tenant taking a new lease or an assignee of an existing lease. In either event the questions to be asked from him are the same as those relating to the buyer of a freehold (see Chapter 2) but the precise terms of the agreement need to be ascertained in more detail so that the buyer is additionally asked:

- How much rent he has agreed to pay and whether after a period of years it is agreed that this will be reviewed?
- The duration of the lease.
- The responsibilities for maintenance, outgoings and insurance.

3.3   Licence to assign a lease

It is the duty of the existing tenant desiring to sell his leasehold interest to the buyer to check from the terms of his lease as to whether or not the landlord's consent is required to the transaction. Generally, the landlord's consent is only required in respect of commercial leases where traditionally the premises are let at an open market rent which is reviewed every three or five years. It is therefore of significance for the landlord to ascertain the means of the proposed assignee so as to satisfy himself that the assignee can afford to pay the rent that may now be payable and in the future may be required.

If the landlord's permission is required the tenant's legal representatives must ask the proposed assignee's legal representative to produce references. A bank reference is always required and it is common for there to be a request for two further references such as trading references or, where none is available, personal references. The references can be taken up either by the proposed assignee's legal representative or by the seller's legal representative. There is a special procedure relating to the taking up of a bank reference. Bank references are supplied from one bank to another and not direct to the applicant. Furthermore, the references are in a form so that initials are used instead of names, and a form of words is employed, the significance of which is clear to the legal representatives involved but which is not otherwise particularly explicit.

Upon receipt of the references these will be despatched to the landlord or to the landlord's legal representative. It is for them to decide whether or not they are satisfied with these references.

Generally, the clause in a business lease requiring the landlord's consent is with the words 'such consent not to be unreasonably withheld'. If the landlord refuses his permission unreasonably, it is possible to challenge that decision in the court in order to force his consent. An unqualified clause giving the landlord an absolute right of veto is rare.

It is not uncommon for the landlord's legal representative to make the landlord's consent conditional. For example, premises may be in a state of disrepair and agreement may be sought to put the premises back into repair before the licence to assign is finalised. Equally it may be that there is a rent review due in the next few months and in such a case the new rent will be agreed at this juncture as part of the discussions which take place at the time of the licence to assign.

A licence to assign is merely a permission from the landlord to the existing tenant enabling him to sell his lease to a proposed assignee. Generally, the licence appears in the form of a deed and this is carefully prepared by the landlord's solicitor and submitted to the tenant's solicitor who in turn submits it to the proposed assignee's solicitor for approval. The deed is drafted and submitted in duplicate. It is not uncommon for the deed to include a direct covenant as between the landlord and the proposed assignee that the proposed assignee will pay the rent agreed and observe all the conditions of the existing lease. Once the draft licence to assign has been approved by those concerned it will be engrossed in duplicate with one copy described as the licence to assign and the other copy described as the counterpart licence to assign. The licence to assign is to be executed by the landlord and the counterpart licence to assign will be executed by the proposed assignee. On completion these two will be exchanged.

3.4   Drafting the contract

This is the task of the seller's solicitor where an existing lease is being assigned, or the landlord's solicitor where a new lease is being granted. The contract will generally be submitted in duplicate for approval together with a copy of the lease. Sometimes a contract is dispensed with on the understanding that the matter remains subject to contract until completion.

The preparation of the contract is the same as mentioned above and below is a note of the differences in terms of preparation:

- The description of the property should accord with the description contained in the lease and it should be expressly stated that the interest sold is leasehold.
- The root of title will be the lease, or, where fifteen years or more have elapsed, an assignment of the lease. The root can be an assignment for value. In practice, the lease itself will be used and this contains the clauses and provisions which govern the entire transaction.
- A further special condition will provide that the property is sold subject to the tenant's covenants in the lease in addition to the restrictive covenants and matters which may be contained in the freehold title which will of course bind the tenant even though he takes the leasehold title.
- The requirement for the tenant to obtain the landlord's licence to assign may also be made a condition of the contract.
- If the sale is not merely of the leasehold estate but also of an existing business the preparation of the contract will be fundamentally different in so far as it will additionally embrace the apportionment of the price as between the leasehold estate, the fixtures and fittings and the goodwill. It will also contain clauses dealing with the assignment of the goodwill and a clause restricting the vendor from competing within a certain radius for a certain period of time.

Where a buyer is buying an existing business it is important to check that the buyer is registered for the purposes of VAT. If the buyer is not registered for VAT purposes he will have to pay VAT on the price, which he could not then recover.

3.5   Preliminary enquiries

The standard form of preliminary enquiries is the same as that which relates to the conveyancing of freeholds but there are a number of additional questions which relate simply to leaseholds.

(1) The vendor is required to disclose whether the transaction involves the sale of a head lease or a sublease. A subtenant is required to comply with any covenants within the head lease whether or not he is actually aware of them and it will therefore be important to show both leases to a proposed buyer of a sublease.

(2) The name and address of the landlord or his solicitors is required.

(3) The landlord may grant a licence to authorise what would other-

wise be a breach of covenant by the tenant. Unless this has been given, the seller will be expected to have observed all the covenants in the lease.

(4) The steps the seller has taken to obtain a licence to assign must be set out in the appropriate cases.

Other additional enquiries relating to leaseholds include the following.

3.5.1 Covenants A complaint by the landlord may take the form of a notice under the Law of Property Act 1925, s 146 which is generally required before a breach of a covenant or condition is enforced. No notice is needed where the rent is in arrears.

A covenant to decorate the premises in a particular calendar year imposes a duty at the beginning of that year and is not avoided because the lease is assigned before the end of it.

In most leases there is an express covenant for quiet enjoyment and where this is not expressly stated, it is implied. Similarly, there are implied repairing covenants by the landlord in residential tenancies granted for less than seven years. Additionally, the landlord will be expected to comply with any other covenants contained in the lease.

3.5.2 Service charges In addition to the rent most leases carry a 'service charge' which is a charge levied for the maintenance of the building, its insurance and other outgoings which cannot be specifically attributed to one particular unit. The service charge accrues from day to day and upon completion of the sale is apportionable on a time basis. The seller will be required to state the date of the last payment and the attempts may have to be made to ascertain from the landlord the current charging rate. Service charges tend to vary from one year to another and that depends on the overall cost of running the building in which any given letting unit is located.

A buyer will enquire whether the seller has exercised the right to obtain information from the landlord concerning the service charge. The tenant can request in writing from the landlord within one year after the end of the calendar year concerned a written summary of the costs affecting his service charge. The landlord is duty bound to comply with the request within one month or six months after the end of the accounting year, whichever is latest.

A statutory right to information does not apply if the tenant is afforded reasonable facilities for inspecting certified accounts giving the same information, if there are no more than five flats in the building and if the tenant is afforded reasonable facilities for inspecting receipts and records. The local authority's housing association, tenants' associations and companies are exempt.

3.5.3 Insurance Where a lease contains a tenant's covenant to insure and the landlord effects the policy, the tenant cannot rely upon the landlord continuing to insure. If the landlord is obliged to insure, ask to see a copy of the policy and ensure that the tenant's interest is subsequently endorsed on it.

3.5.4 Reversions The seller of an existing lease is simply required to deduce title which will enable the buyer to register the lease at HM Land Registry with an absolute title or would enable him to do so if the title to the lease was registrable. Pursuant to the provisions of the Standard Conditions of Sale (First Edition) the same applies in respect of new leases and this effectively means that the buyer of a leasehold estate is now entitled to see the freehold title.

3.6   Dealing with a management company

Sometimes a landlord of a block of flats or even of a large Victorian house which has been divided into flats may not wish to retain the ongoing responsibility for the building after he has granted all the leases. In such cases, it is common for the leases granted to be for a period in excess of ninety-nine years in which case leases will be sold for a considerable premium and will merely be subject to a small annual ground rent together with the annual service charges. Accordingly, the landlord's investment in the freehold reversion is very small indeed and there is little advantage to him in retaining the ongoing responsibility of the building. The landlord may therefore establish a management company which will be a private limited company in respect of which each new tenant will be required to obtain one or more shares. The purchase of these shares at a nominal price is likely to be made a special condition of the contract.

Each tenant of each flat will then become a member of the management company and they will agree among themselves as to who the directors and secretary should be. They will meet in order to decide matters of expenditure, the lighting and the heating of the common parts of the building, the decorating of passageways and the maintenance of any garden areas.

The management company will be required to comply with provisions of the Companies Acts and where tenants are unable to cope with this responsibility themselves additional service charges will be incurred in seeking professional assistance.

Sometimes the management company will have the freehold reversion transferred to it so that the management company additionally receives the ground rent. Arrangements for this vary.

With regard to business premises, control and maintenance of the building generally remains in the hands of the landlord. Here the leases are not granted for lengthy periods and twenty-one or forty years would be the longest period in respect of which one would expect to find a lease. These leases are not bought or sold for significant premiums and as a consequence an open market rent is charged which generally runs into thousands of pounds per annum and this rent is reviewed periodically in accordance with extensive provisions set out in a standard form of lease.

3.7 Deducing title

The legal representative acting for a buyer of a leasehold interest will scrutinise replies to preliminary enquiries, undertake searches, examine the search results, raise any further enquiries which are necessary, report to his client with regard to the details of his findings and, if so instructed, approve the contract and exchange contracts. All this occurs in the same way as the conveyancing of a freehold and on exchange of contracts it will be necessary for the seller's solicitor to deduce title if he has not previously done so.

Where the transaction involves the assignment of an existing lease, the title will comprise the lease and the subsequent assignments. There may be mortgages and should be land charge search results. The epitome of title is prepared in the same way as described in 2.10 and submitted to the buyer's legal representatives for their perusal.

Where the transaction involves the grant of a new lease it is likely the lease will have been agreed before contracts were exchanged and in those circumstances the task remaining after contracts are exchanged is for the landlord's solicitor to engross the deed in duplicate. The superior title should be deduced.

3.8 Raising requisitions on title

The standard form of requisitions is the same as that employed for freeholds but certain additional questions apply to leaseholds.

The seller is requested to supply receipts for the outgoings and in particular the last receipt for rent paid to the landlord. This receipt is of significance because it implies that there are no outstanding breaches of the tenant's covenant under the lease.

The seller is requested to supply the name and address of the person who should be supplied with a notice of the transaction (usually the head landlord). Notice should be served within a stipulated period of time and in respect of which a small fee is likely to be required. This is the responsibility of the assignee's legal representative and the client pays the fee.

As with a freehold property there may be defects with the title. There may be a missing assignment or missing search results or one of the assignments may not have been properly stamped by the Inland Revenue. If any of these or other eventualities occurs, additional requisitions should be raised so that there is a perfect title on completion.

3.9   Drafting a deed of assignment

A deed of assignment of an existing lease has the same effect as a deed of conveyance for an existing freehold. The format of the deed is very similar to a conveyance.

The following points should be noted:

- If a recital clause is included, it should recite the original lease together with any subsequent assignments.
- The description of the property in the parcels clause should accord with that contained within the lease and it should be made clear that the leasehold estate is being transferred.
- The assignee should undertake to observe the covenants as appropriate but there will be no need for an acknowledgement for production clause as the original lease and assignments would be handed over on completion. The sale of part of a leasehold property would amount to a sublease. In this respect a new lease would have been prepared thereby obviating the need for a deed of assignment.

The deed of assignment is prepared by the buyer's legal representative and is submitted for approval by the seller's representative. It is submitted in duplicate and the engrossment is then signed by the buyer and returned to the seller's representative for signature by his client in readiness for completion. The deed is dated on the day of completion.

If the leasehold interest is to be the subject of first registration the deed of assignment can be replaced by a simple transfer deed pursuant to the land registration rules. With effect from 31 July 1990, a requirement for deeds to be sealed where they are executed by an individual, is abolished. All that is required is for the parties' signatures to be witnessed and attested. The appropriate attestation clause may now have the words 'signed as a Deed' in order to validate the document as a deed. This change is pursuant to s 1 of the Law of Property (Miscellaneous Provisions) Act 1989. Changes in the law relating to the execution of deeds by companies are made by s 130 of the Companies Act 1989 and will also be brought into effect on 31 July 1990. Directors may now sign on behalf of a company, avoiding the need for a company seal.

3.10   Making arrangements for completion

The seller's legal representative must check that he is in possession of the executed deed of assignment or the new lease duly executed by his client.

They will contact the buyer's representative in order to set up arrangements for completion which may either be through the post as before or at the seller's solicitor's office. They will have previously supplied a completion statement which is more important when dealing with leaseholds as it will include the apportionment of any rent and service charges.

The buyer's legal representative will ensure that he has collected sufficient funds for completion and he will have previously sent his own statement to his client in order to collect the sums due.

In addition to any purchase price he may have to pay rent for the next rent period provided by the lease. Rent is only payable in advance where it is expressly stated in the lease, otherwise the presumption is that it is paid in arrears. Appropriate arrangements will be made on completion depending on the circumstances.

Postal completion may not be possible by using the immediate money transfer (IMT) system between banks where the total to be transferred is less than £10,000. This threshold varies slightly but it is important to check it because if it is not possible to send the money on the day of completion, arrangements should be made to ensure funds are available a few days earlier and that a banker's draft can be prepared or a client account cheque sent. Banks may charge for an IMT. This should be added as a disbursement to the client's completion statement.

3.11   Post-completion formalities

The buyer's legal representative should collect the deeds and documents and compare these with the copies forming part of the epitome. He should also send the deed of assignment to the Inland Revenue for stamping in accordance with the procedure described before.

A leasehold estate is registrable where the lease has at least forty years to run or is for twenty-one years and the superior title is registered.

The seller's legal representative should, upon collecting the proceeds of sale, ensure that the landlord no longer turns to his client for payment of future rent and service charges and further he should disburse the proceeds of sale in accordance with the agreement reached with the client as set out on the completion statement which the client will by now have approved.

CHAPTER 4

REGISTERED CONVEYANCING: FREEHOLDS AND LEASEHOLDS

4.1 Dealing with first registration

The procedure of conveying registered land is very similar to that dealing with unregistered land and this is particularly true in respect of the pre-contract formalities. In these circumstances the reader is referred to Chapter 2 on handling unregistered freeholds.

The system of registered conveyancing was introduced by the Land Registration Act 1925 and the aim was to simplify conveyancing procedure. This means that on the transfer of certain legal estates the estate becomes registrable at the successful conclusion of the dealing. Failure to register prevents the estate from passing. Registration is performed by a number of district Land Registries each being responsible for certain counties. Upon application being made to them they will issue a certificate to the proprietor of the land or mortgagee and this will replace all the old title deeds.

The certificate is legal proof of title. Where there is no mortgage it will be described as a land certificate and where there is a mortgage it will be described as a charge certificate. If there is more than one mortgage each mortgagee will have his own certificate. The subsequent certificates will however be impressed on the front cover with a green seal instead of a red seal.

Once land is registered it is always registered. In general it is not possible to register the ownership of land situated in non-compulsory areas. There are exceptions to this basic rule, eg building estates which comprise twenty or more house plots and the purchase of council houses by their tenants pursuant to the provisions of the Housing Act 1985.

In respect of unregistered land in a compulsory area the conveyance or dealing will take place as for unregistered land up to completion. Thereafter there are certain additional registration formalities to be complied with.

Application for first registration in respect of freeholds is made by a representative acting on behalf of the buyer on form 1B. The following information is required to complete this:

- The county and district in which the property is situated.
- A short description of the property.
- Name and address of representative lodging the application and any alternative address for the despatch of requisitions which may be necessary or the return of the certificate at the conclusion of the registration.
- Name and address of the buyer to be registered as the proprietor of the estate in the land together with the details of the documents inducing first registration.
- Value of the land is to be stated as it is upon this that the land registration fee is assessed. Land registration fees were reviewed with effect from 2 April 1990 by the Land Registration Fee Order 1990.
- The capacity of the buyer must be stated as sole beneficial owner, joint tenants or tenants in common.
- The form must state that the legal representative has thoroughly investigated the title and any entries revealed by search result must be expressly set out. Similarly, a note of any subsisting leases which affect the freehold title must be made and a note of any subsisting encumbrances should also appear. The most common encumbrance is a new mortgage; full details must be supplied.

The following must accompany the application form 1B to the appropriate Land Registry:

- A cheque for the necessary fee made payable to HM Land Registry.
- All the deeds and documents of title together with search results, replies to preliminary enquiries, replies to requisitions and the contract relating to the current transaction. These deeds and documents are listed on form A13 which is a preprinted schedule for the listing of the deeds and documents in chronological order. Form A13 is submitted in triplicate.
- The conveyance deed or transfer deed inducing first registration together with the buyer's mortgage deed should be accompanied by photocopies duly certified by a properly qualified member of the firm as a true copy of the original deeds. Instead of the conveyance deed it is possible to use a statutory form of transfer pursuant to rule 72 and some representatives prefer this as it obviates the more tedious task of drafting a conveyance deed.

The above documents are submitted to HM Land Registry who will acknowledge safe receipt on one of the forms A13. On that form they will also indicate the new title number allotted to the property together with an estimate of the period of time it will take to complete the registration. This period will vary from one district Land Registry to another. It is possible to pay an expedition fee of £25 in order to accelerate the registration and if the property is to be sold quickly such payment may be helpful.

The certificate will be returned by the Land Registry together with a notice of completion of the registration and at that stage the certificate should be carefully checked for spelling mistakes or other matters which appear to be incorrect. If there are errors, these will be put right by the Land Registry quickly without charge.

The unregistered deeds and documents will be returned but in order to prevent those unregistered deeds from being used wrongly they will be stamped with a rectangular stamp by the Land Registry indicating that they are no longer valid in themselves. Some regard it as good practice to retain the unregistered deeds because if queries have to be answered in the future it may provide greater detail in respect of certain covenants or restrictions affecting the property. On the other hand many building societies urge practitioners not to send them the unregistered deeds and documents because it adds unnecessarily to the cost of postage and storage.

The charge certificate must be returned to the mortgagee. A land certificate can be retained in the firm's strongroom or otherwise stored in accordance with the client's instructions.

Application for first registration of a leasehold estate is made on form 2B. The lease will not be retained in the Land Registry but will be returned with the certificate to the applicant's solicitors.

4.1.1 The certificate and its registers The certificate is correct as of the date it is issued. The date that it is 'last compared' is stamped on the inside cover of the certificate. At that date it accords with the central registry records. Subsequently, it may become out of date so that the central registry records are different from the actual certificate. Copies of recent application and changes may be applied for either by undertaking a Land Registry search (form 94A) or by requesting office copy entries (form A44 or A44A). The certificate itself is divided up into three registers.

The *property register* contains the title number, the description of the land by reference to the filed plan which is based on the ordnance survey and its postal address. Also contained here are easements such as rights of way or rights of drainage and exceptions and reservations. Easements, exceptions and reservations and declarations and other similar matters may not be set out in full in the property register but may be referred to by reference to a deed or document which has been incorporated with the certificate generally at the back. This is particularly common practice when dealing with the sale of property on a new housing estate.

Matters described as 'overriding interests' are exempted from first registration. These are fully set out in the Land Registration Act 1925, s 70 and include such matters as rights of persons in actual occupation of the land.

The *proprietorship register* sets out the type of title together with the name and address of the registered proprietor. Any restrictions on the right of the registered proprietor to deal with the property freely or to receive the proceeds of sale will also be set out, possibly preceded by the words 'Notice' or 'Caution'.

The *charges register* contains all incumbrances which burden the land. It includes such matters as subsisting mortgages, notices of deposit and restrictive covenants. Again the mortgage deed will be sewn into the back of this certificate and restrictive covenants may be contained in the transfer deed which is sewn into the certificate.

There are two types of title as follows:

- Absolute title is the best title. The registered proprietor is the owner of the fee simple subject only to any overriding interests.
- Qualified title is the same as an absolute title except that land is held subject to any claims against the land which arise before registration. It is available for someone with possession like a squatter where there appears to be no legal owner.

With regard to a leasehold title, the best title is an absolute title but is only available where both freehold and leasehold have been investigated by the land registrar.

Good leasehold title is given where the title is approved by the registrar without investigation of the freehold title.

4.2   Drafting the contract

The preparation of the contract is the same as for a contract in respect of registered freehold and remains the obligation of the seller's solicitors. However, there are two differences.

First, the description of the property should closely follow the description contained in the land certificate. For example, the following might be appropriate:

> ALL THAT freehold property known as No 12 Jones Street, Barset Town, Barsetshire as the same is registered at HM Land Registry with Title Number UK121212 with title absolute

TOGETHER WITH the easements contained or referred to in the property register for the said title number.

Secondly, a most fundamental difference is that it is no longer necessary to seek a root of title which is fifteen years old or more as with unregistered conveyancing. Instead, standard condition 4 commits the seller to deduce title in accordance with s 110 of the Land Registration Act 1925 and requires the seller to produce office copy entries so that the buyer may ascertain for himself the present position with regard to the title. In this way the inspection of the title takes place before contracts are exchanged and can be done far more speedily and easily because it avoids the need to examine an epitome containing a series of deeds and documents.

4.3 Preliminary enquiries

The procedure whereby the buyer's solicitor undertakes his local authority search is the same as for unregistered conveyancing. An index map search is not applicable for registered land and neither is a land charges search from the land charges department in Plymouth. The procedure of raising preliminary enquiries is the same for unregistered conveyancing although there are questions which apply to registered land and not to unregistered land. For example, question 8B on the specimen form set out in Chapter 8 asks if there are any overriding interests. Additional preliminary enquiries may be raised as a result of what one has seen from the office copy entries. Strictly speaking, preliminary enquiries are not enquiries about the title of the property which is generally dealt with as part of raising requisitions.

4.4 Deducing title

The seller's representative will generally acquire the charge certificate from the seller's mortgagee prior to preparing and despatching a draft contract and this certificate is the totality of the title required in most cases. To update the title he will apply for office copy entries on form A44 or A44A. The fee for these is £12 or £6 for part only, eg title plan. The legal representative is obliged to complete details of the property on the form and he specifies his own authority to inspect the title. The representative making the application for office copies must decide whether he requires any or all of the documents referred to in the certificate. New arrangements provide for immediate despatch of office copies and an additional request for office copy documents on form A44A will be processed separately.

Office copies are distinct from ordinary photocopies so far as they are on Crown watermarked paper. Care must be taken to avoid photocopies being passed off as official copies. Office copy plans use the following colour references:

- Red edging to show the extent of the registered land.
- Green edging to indicate the land removed from a title.
- Green tinting to show excluded islands of land within the land edged red.
- Brown tinting for the part of the registered land subject to a right of way.

4.5   Land registration search

A land registration search is despatched to the appropriate district Land Registry for the area in which the property is situated and is carried out on Land Registry form 94A (see Chapter 8) where the transaction involves the sale of the whole of the land comprised in a registered title or form 94B where the sale only relates to part of the land in a registered title. In both cases the form must be completed with details of the county and district in which the property is situated, its title number, the name of the registered proprietor and the identity of the applicant. Where one acts for a mortgagee as well as for the borrower, the applicant will be the mortgagee.

It is also important to state the dates from which the search is required. Where an office copy has been issued, the date of issue of the office copy will be the date from which the search is required. If this is not so, the date on which the certificate was last compared with the register is the date from which the search should be undertaken.

Where the transaction involves the purchase of part it may be that form 102, being a certificate of inspection of the filed plan, has been issued by the Land Registry to the developer's representatives. If this is so, the plot number and the date on which it is approved is the only information required to undertake the search. Otherwise a plan would be required to be submitted with the search form 94B. The forms are submitted in duplicate and the search result is returned on the back of one of the forms in form 94D. This states whether or not there have been any dealings with the property since the date searches and if there have these must be carefully scrutinised before proceeding further. If there have been no dealings or those dealings which have taken place have not affected the current transaction, the matter proceeds to completion. There is a period of priority of thirty working days afforded by the result of this search and this period is defined by the Land Registration (Official Searches) Rules

1986 (SI No 1536). This information is stamped on the search result and generally gives six clear calendar weeks. If this period should expire before completion has taken place, a further search will be necessary.

Applicants wishing to make a search by telephone or telex may do so through their legal representative. Where a credit account is held, the key number and reference should be included in any telex application made after 2 April 1990. Non-credit account holders should hold an undertaking to pay the fee. Legal representatives making a search by telephone on or after 2 April 1990 will be asked to give this undertaking, or if they hold a credit account, their key number and reference.

The Land Registry forms are in the course of being re-designed, but Land Registry form 105 has been revised in order to assist with the arrangements which were devised with effect from the above date.

Apart from a search in the Land Registry prior to completion, it will be necessary to undertake a bankruptcy search against the names of the proposed buyers where they are raising a mortgage. This search is undertaken on the land charges form K16 which is sent to the Land Charges Dept at Plymouth.

4.6 Raising requisitions on title

The procedure follows that relating to unregistered freeholds so that after the contracts are exchanged the buyer's representative prepares a draft transfer in duplicate and submits this for approval with requisitions on title, also in duplicate. The standard form is the same as the standard form relating to unregistered land but as with the standard form of preliminary enquiries there are questions which are pertinent and others which are not, in respect of registered land.

Requisition 3A will be inapplicable and 3B will apply. Part I requires the date, the certificate was last compared with the register to be stated and Parts 2 and 3 ask if an estate layout plan has been approved and if the seller's certificate was on deposit at the Land Registry. These two parts only relate to sales of part of the land comprised in a title where, eg, a new house is being sold by a developer.

Secondly, where dealing with the sale of part of land comprised in a registered title, the usual practice is for the seller's solicitor to put the seller's certificate on deposit at the Land Registry. A deposit number is then allotted and, when each buyer makes application to register his particular property ownership, the deposit number is stated instead of submitting the certificate on each separate occasion.

4.7   Drafting the transfer deed

This is the task of the buyer's solicitor and this takes the place of a conveyance of unregistered land. There is a series of transfer forms and most practitioners select the appropriate form for the transaction they are dealing with. Sometimes it is necessary to draft a transfer deed without using a standard form and this is particularly necessary when dealing with an estate development. In such a case the seller's solicitor will prepare a standard deed for use on all occasions and this deed will have to be accepted as it stands because alterations are likely to have consequences for the neighbours.

Some of the more commonly used forms are as follows:

- Forms 19 and 32A: freehold and leasehold title from one sole owner to another.
- Forms 19CO and 32ACO: where the seller is a company.
- Form 35: where the buyer is a company.
- Form 19JP: where the parties to the transaction are joint owners.
- Form 20: where part only is to be transferred.
- Form 43: where new restrictive covenants are to be imposed. This is a longer form for use in the sale of an individual property but comprising only part of that obtained in a title. Such a transfer should be accompanied by a plan which is signed by both parties to the transaction.

There is sufficient room on the pre-printed forms to insert an indemnity covenant whereby a buyer agrees to indemnify the seller against any breach of any covenants which the buyer fails to observe after completing his purchase, thereby causing the seller loss.

Where there are two or more buyers, there is a standard clause which needs to be completed to indicate whether the survivor of them could give a good receipt to a future buyer. Basically, if the parties hold as beneficial joint tenants as most husbands and wives will, then the survivor will be able to give a good receipt. This may not be the case where the buyers hold as tenants in common, but this would be more likely to refer to business situations.

In the absence of an indemnity clause or a joint tenancy clause it may not be necessary for the buyers to sign a deed of transfer. It will be necessary for them to sign in order to give effect to either of the above two clauses.

Where the value of the property passing is below the exempt limit for the purposes of payment of stamp duty, the certificate of value should be inserted in order to avoid duty being paid at the rate of 1% of the purchase price.

At the time of writing the threshold is £30,000.00. The revised arrangements for signing a deed with effect from 31 July 1990 have been explained above.

4.8 Post-completion formalities

4.8.1 Seller's representative He will make arrangements for completion and after completion will proceed in the same way as for a completion for unregistered conveyancing. However, the procedure for discharging the subsisting mortgage is slightly different. The mortgagee will be required to sign or seal a form 53. This form must be filled out using the information contained in the charge certificate as to the date of the charge and date it was registered. It is important that the seller's representative does not part with the charge certificate until he has completed form 53 and despatched it for signing or sealing by the mortgagee together with a cheque for the necessary amount to redeem the subsisting mortgage.

The seller's representative will have given an undertaking to the purchaser's representative to remit the duly completed form 53 as soon as it is returned to him by the mortgagee.

4.8.2 Buyer's representative Upon completion he will collect the charge certificate and any ancillary papers such as planning permissions, guarantee certificates and miscellaneous documents from the seller's representative. The transfer deed will be dated with the day of completion and if the transaction involves more than £30,000 (the current threshold for stamp duty) it will need to be sent to the Inland Revenue with the stamps form for stamping. The procedure is the same as previously described.

With regard to transactions involving £30,000 or less it is now possible for the Land Registry to deal with the stamping formalities themselves and the stamps form LA451 must be duly completed and despatched with the transfer deed and the other deeds and documents required by the Land Registry in order to deal with the registration. In effect, the Registry then deals with both the adjudication of the deed when no stamp duty is payable and then the registration of the new proprietor as the owner of the land. Registration of a dealing, in other words with land which is already registered, is performed by completing Land Registry form A4. A copy of this is contained in Chapter 8. The form needs to be completed with the county and district in which the property is situated together with the property's address and title number. The nature and priority of applications must be noted and where the seller has had to redeem a mortgage, this should be stated first. Thereafter, the transfer of the land should be mentioned together with the consideration passing under the transfer deed and it is on this basis that the land registration fee is payable. Third will be the buyer's new mortgage, and where this is registered simultaneously with change of ownership, there is no additional fee payable.

Form A4 further requires details and the address of the applicant's representative together with details of the applicant's name and the address of any new mortgagee together with a statement as to whether the survivor of joint tenants can give a receipt of the proceeds of sale. The application form must be signed by a suitably qualified member of the firm and despatched together with the appropriate fee. The buyer's representative must also despatch the following which are listed on form A4:

- charge certificate
- form 53
- transfer deed
- mortgage deed
- certified copy mortgage deed.

On despatch of the above to the appropriate Land Registry a postcard acknowledgement is likely to be received stipulating how long the land registration is likely to take. When the charge certificate is returned duly amended and incorporating the new mortgage deed, it should be checked before being despatched to the mortgagee.

CHAPTER 5

TRANSACTION

5.1 Introduction

The National Protocol has been designed by the Law Society for use in domestic conveyancing of freehold and leasehold property. Its use is voluntary, and at the outset of any given transaction, it must be explained to and accepted by the proposed seller as soon as he decides to place his property on the market and it must subsequently be accepted by the legal representatives acting for the buyer. Because the use of TransAction is voluntary and at the time of writing only just beginning to emerge, the practitioner must be familiar with the traditional system of conveyancing as described above.

That system is likely to prevail for commercial property for the time being. TransAction simplifies conveyancing procedures and is designed to speed up the conveyancing process so as to make conveyancing commercially attractive to the new client. In reality the new system does not represent a departure from the old procedures. It simply breaks those procedures down to a more simple and straightforward form and the marketing literature put forward by the Law Society for solicitors and clients, should enable solicitors to compete effectively with others who may now enter the conveyancing market.

Even if the National Protocol is adopted between solicitors, there is the right to give notice to the solicitor acting for the other party of a decision to depart from one or more of the Protocol procedures. The interests of the client remain paramount. The Law Society itself provides the prescribed forms but the standard conditions of sale contract may be obtained from law stationers.

5.2 Acting for the seller

The seller should consult his chosen solicitor when he puts the property on the market. Estate Agents should be made aware of this change in procedure. The seller's solicitor should obtain the deeds as described above and should proceed to undertake a local authority search at the seller's expense. Any other searches deemed appropriate should be undertaken by the seller's solicitor. This should cut down on the delay involved with the buyer's solicitor undertaking the searches.

The client should be asked to complete the 'property information questionnaire'. On the front cover this warns the seller that he should supply truthful answers to the practical questions which are set out inside the booklet. The questions are more or less identical to those contained on the Preliminary Enquiries form, but they are set out according to a more modern and practical style. When the client has completed the booklet and signed it, it should be returned to the seller's solicitor who will then be able to fill in the 'Property Information form' (see Chapter 8). The Property Information form is signed by the seller's solicitor. This again is a simplified form of Preliminary Enquiries, and cuts out the use of ever lengthening forms of Enquiries Before Contract. Additionally, at this initial stage, the seller must be asked to complete the 'Fixtures Fittings and Contents form'. Again, this is a simplified form indicating which fixtures, fittings and contents are included or excluded, or in the latter case if there are none at the property. The seller is requested to tick the appropriate boxes and to indicate at the bottom of that form the total price agreed for what is included. Again, the seller should sign this form, and the form should be forwarded by the seller's solicitor to the buyer's solicitor with the contract, of which it will form part.

The 'Contract for Sale' incorporates the new standard conditions of sale which have been variously referred to earlier in the text. These are a simplified version of the earlier Law Society and National Conditions of Sale.

The seller's solicitor will despatch the following to the buyer's solicitor at the commencement of a new transaction.

- The Local Authority Search and any other relevant search results.
- The Contract for Sale.
- The Property Information form.
- The Fixtures, Fittings and Contents form.
- Evidence of title, dependent on whether the property is registered or unregistered.

5.3   Acting for the buyer

The buyer's solicitor should receive a comprehensive package of information about the property and this places him in a good position to report fully to his client at the outset. The new system therefore avoids the customary delay incurred in waiting for a local authority search result, and dealing with Enquiries Before Contract.

However, the buyer's solicitor is still obliged to use his professional skill, knowledge, and judgement and he is entitled to be dissatisfied with the package received in order to protect his own client. For example, the Protocol does not reverse the *caveat emptor* rule. Similarly, it is up to the buyer's solicitor to decide whether the searches obtained by the seller's solicitor are adequate for the buyer's purposes. This point is underlined in the new conditions of sale.

5.4   Exchanging contracts

When the buyer's solicitor is satisfied and when his client has obtained the necessary mortgage finance, and generally made the necessary progress in respect of any related transaction, Contracts can be exchanged precisely as described previously in this work. Sometimes, the period between exchange of contracts and completion may be very short, and the delivery of a draft transfer/conveyance may be helpful, prior to exchange of contracts. Sometimes, the seller's solicitor may provide such a draft document as part of the initial package. The effect of s 3 of the Law of Property (Miscellaneous Provisions) Act 1989 repealing the rule in *Bain* v *Fothergill* is to encourage solicitors to stipulate in the contract that the title is to be accepted. This means that the buyer's solicitors may raise their requisitions in advance of the Protocol time table (See Chapter 6.1).

The emphasis in the Protocol scheme is on simplicity, speed and efficiency.

5.5   The remaining formalities

Save as described above, all other conveyancing formalities as set out in this work are the same as under the old system.

If dealing with licensed conveyancers, there is no reason why they should not be invited to operate the Law Society Protocol system.

5.6   Marketing

A client pack may be purchased by solicitors in order to explain the operation of the system to clients. Solicitors are encouraged to supply the pack at the outset of the transaction and it is suggested that the clients should file their own correspondence about the transaction in the pack. Where appropriate, solicitors might provide the client with the copies of searches and the Property Information form and of the title deeds or copy entries. These can also be kept in the pack, assisting the client in the aim to make more visible the work being done by the solicitor. After completion, the aim is that a client should keep the pack to act as a reminder of the solicitor he used and of the service given.

5.7   Conclusion

The development of the Protocol is envisaged to be evolutionary so that changes and adjustments might be expected as practitioners become more experienced in dealing with it. For further information about the operation of the Protocol, and for copies of the forms and literature referred to above, practitioners should apply to the Law Society

CHAPTER 6

TIME LIMITS

6.1 Stipulations by the Standard Conditions of Sale (First Edition)

(1) Unless fixed by the contract, completion date is twenty working days after the date of the contract, but time is not of the essence of the contract unless a notice to complete has been served.

(2) If the money due on completion is received after 2.00pm, completion is to be treated as taking place on the next working day, and this means that interest at the contract rate is payable on the outstanding balance purchase money.

(3) In apportioning any sum, it is assumed that the seller owns the property until the end of the day from which the apportionment is made, and that the sum accrues from day to day at the rate at which it is payable on that day. This commonly relates to the community charge or water rates.

It is assumed that such outgoings accrue at an equal daily rate throughout the year and where any sums to be apportioned are not known on the actual completion day, apportionment is to be made according to the best estimate available. As soon after completion as the amount is known, a final apportionment is to be made, and notified to the other party and any resulting balance paid, no more than ten working days later.

(4) The contract provides a timetable for dealing with evidence of title and preparation of the transfer deed. The seller must send the buyer evidence of title immediately after making the contract. The buyer may raise written requisitions six working days after either the date of the contract or the day of delivery of the seller's evidence of title on which the requisitions are raised, whichever is the later. The seller is to reply in writing to requisitions raised four working days after receiving them. The buyer may make written observations on the seller's replies within three working days after receiving the replies. The buyer's right to raise requisitions or make observations is lost after the expiration of the relevant time limit.

With regard to the transfer deed, the buyer is to send the seller a draft transfer at least twelve working days before the completion date. The seller is to approve or revise that draft and either return it or retain it for use as the actual transfer within four working days after the delivery of the draft. If the draft is returned, the buyer is to send an engrossment to the seller at least five working days before the completion date. The periods of time in respect of dealing with the title and in respect of dealing with the transfer deed may run concurrently. If the period between the date of the contract, and completion is less than fifteen working days, the time limits are reduced by the same proportion as that period bears to the period of fifteen working days. Fractions of a working day are to be rounded down, except that the time limit to perform any step is not to be less than one working day.

(5) Where a party is unable to complete on the appointed day, condition 6.6 provides that a notice to complete should be served upon the defaulting party and ten working days is afforded by this condition within which period completion must be effected. If not, legal action for breach of contract can be instituted, and the position here is set out by standard conditions 7.5 and 7.6.

A more ample exposition of the standard conditions of sale is set out by Frances Silverman, Solicitor, Principal Lecturer at the College of Law in the third edition of her Conveyancers Guide, published by Format Publishing.

6.2   Durability of search results

6.2.1 Local land charges search   The result of a local land charges search was treated as valid for a period of two months after the date of the search result. However, to remove the problems associated with the length of time upon which the result of a local search can be relied, the Law Society has arranged an insurance policy to be used in the case of any residential property where the purchase price does not exceed £500,000.00 and where the date of exchange of contracts is not more than six months from the date of the result of the most recent search on the property. The insurance covers the buyer and the buyer's lender. It provides indemnity for the difference in the market value of the property at the time of exchange of contracts caused by an adverse entry arising between the date of the result of the earlier search and the date of exchange of contracts. The cover is up to the limit of indemnity under the insurance which limit is the purchase price of the property. The premium is apparently £10.00 if the purchase price does not exceed £250,000.00 and £20.00 if the purchase price is between £250,000.00 and £500,000.00. The Scheme administrators are Legal and Professional Indemnity Ltd, P O Box 213, Tunbridge Wells, Kent, TN3 0LT (DX 3923 TUN-BRIDGE WELLS).

Under TransAction (see *post*) the seller is responsible for undertaking a local authority search at his own cost and such a move minimises subsequent delays in the conveyancing procedures.

6.2.2 Land charges search Where there is inadequate time to post a land charge search request, it is possible to search on the telephone by telephoning the Land Charges Department at Plymouth between the hours of 10.00 am and 4.00 pm. It will be necessary to request a telephone search and then to give the firm's key number so that the cost can be allocated to the firm's account. The names of the parties, period of years and county will have to be quoted as if they were being placed on form K15. The result of the search will be given there and then and the result will subsequently be posted. The cost of this facility is £2 per name. Facsimile transmissions are similarly possible as described above.

The result of these searches contains the date at the top of the result. The priority period conferred is also noted at the top and this will be a period of twenty-one days from the date of the search. Completion should be effected within the priority period conferred by the search result in order to protect the transaction from any intervening applications to register matters against the names of the sellers.

6.2.3 Land registration searches Land registration searches forms 94A and 94B confer a priority period of thirty working days (six weeks) in which period completion should occur. The transfer deed should be stamped by the Inland Revenue, and the application be made to the appropriate district Land Registry. In certain cases this can be a tight schedule but it is one which should be met particularly bearing in mind that in the majority of cases one acts for the mortgagee as well as for the buyer. If it is impossible to meet this schedule, Rule 95 provides for the situation whereby the application can be recorded by the Land Registry prior to stamping by the Inland Revenue.

It is advisable to despatch all search requests by first class post. The results will follow quickly also by first class post.

As described above searches can also be made by telephone or telex.

6.3 Application to the Inland Revenue for stamping deeds

6.3.1 Conveyances and transfer deeds Stamp duty applying to conveyance deeds and transfer deeds is currently dealt with by the

Finance Act 1984, s 109 which applies to all instruments executed on or after 20 March 1984. The rate of stamp duty payable is 1 per cent of the purchase price in respect of all those transactions involving £30,000 or more. Exemption on considerations up to £30,000 is conditional on the inclusion in the instrument of an appropriate certificate of value.

Certain instruments are exempt from stamp duty totally and these are prescribed by the Stamp Duty (Exempt Instruments) Regulations 1987 (SI No 516). In respect of purchases of houses at a discount from eg local authorities completed on or after 23 March 1981 duty is payable only on the actual discounted price paid. This is also the basis on which the land registration fee is payable. Section 110 of the Finance Act 1984 extended the list of bodies to which the Finance Act 1981 applies so that it includes sales to a tenant by a housing association. Otherwise all sales at a discount are liable to come to the attention of the appropriate district valuer who will then take it upon himself to inspect the property in order to decide on the actual valuation. It is on this valuation that stamp duty may subsequently be claimed by the Inland Revenue.

Instruments in favour of a charity, heritage or memorial fund are exempt from stamp duty but must bear a stamp denoting this (Finance Act 1982, s 129).

Mortgage deeds do not attract stamp duty.

Application for stamping a document should be made within twenty-eight days of the date of the document. A delay beyond that period may incur the payment of additional duty known as penalty duty. The Inland Revenue has a discretion as to the amount to levy.

6.3.2   Leases and agreements for leases   These must be submitted to the Inland Revenue for the purpose of stamping in the same way as a conveyance or transfer deed. The same time limit applies. The amount of duty payable depends on the rent and the period of the lease.

Where the rent is variable the average annual rent for the residue of the term from the date of the execution is taken.

A lease granted for a fixed term granted thereafter until determined is treated as for a definite term equal to the fixed term together with such further period as must elapse before the earliest date at which the lease can be determined.

With regard to premiums which are paid in addition to the rent, if the rent is not over £300 per annum, the instrument is certified at £30,000 and there is no duty payable on the premium. Otherwise it is charged a duty at 1 per cent rounded up to the nearest pound. Where the rent exceeds £300 per annum the whole premium is charged with duty at 1 per cent rounded up to the nearest pound. If the premium is £500 or less the duty is rounded up to the nearest £0.50.

6.4 Application to the Land Registry to register the transfer of the legal estate

The time limit applicable to such applications depends on whether application is for first registration or for registration of a dealing. First registration must be applied for within two months of the date of completion otherwise the legal estate will not pass to the buyer. In the case of dealing with registered land which has been protected by an official search under the Land Registration (Official Searches) Rules 1986 (SI No 1536) the application must be sent to the registry within thirty working days of the search result in order to obtain priority conferred by that result.

CHAPTER 7

FEES

7.1 Search fees

7.1.1 Local land charges search/local authority search The current fees for Part 1 of a Local Authority search are £22.30. The current fee for an official search of the whole of the register is £3.70. This is usually submitted together with a request for a search in the local land charges department and the aggregate fee is £26.00. The cheque should be payable to the appropriate district council or London borough.

Where it is thought appropriate to ask questions in Part 2 of the local authority search the appropriate boxes should be crossed and an additional fee of £1.80 per question will be payable.

It is possible to ask questions which are not contained on the forms and in this case £4.20 will be payable per question.

A personal search is possible at some local authorities and costs an extra £5.00.

The above charges are as recommended by the Association of District Councils and may vary.

7.1.2 A commons registration search A commons registration search costs £6.00, a sum which is payable to the appropriate county council.

7.1.3 Land charges searches The fee is £1.00 per name for a postal search and £2.00 per name for a telephone, teleprinter or facsimile application.

Application for an office copy of an entry in the register including any plan costs £1.00 per copy.

The registration renewal rectification or cancellation of an entry in the register is £1.00 per name and the certificate of cancellation is also £1.00 per name.

7.1.4 Company searches Company searches are generally conducted by using the services of a law stationer and their charges will depend on the extent of the search required. A conveyancing company search stops short of a full search of the register and the approximate cost will amount to £11.00 per company. Before making such a search, check with the stationer whom you are requesting to do the work.

7.2 Land Registry applications

7.2.1 First registration The Land Registration Fee Order 1990 prescribes the registration fees payable on application for the first registration of legal title. This replaces the Land Registration Fee Order 1988.

FORMS AND PRECEDENTS

1982 EDITION

To be submitted in duplicate

REQUISITION FOR
ENQUIRIES OF
DISTRICT COUNCILS
(NOT LONDON BOROUGHS)

NAME AND ADDRESS OF DISTRICT COUNCIL (IN BLOCK LETTERS) TO WHICH THIS FORM IS TO BE SENT
JONESBOROUGH DISTRICT COUNCIL 2 HIGH STREET JONESBOROUGH BROWNSHIRE

Description of the Property

RE 72 Black Horse Lane

Jonesborough

Relevant roadways, footpaths and footways (see Enquiry 1) in addition to those specified in the above address, on which information is sought.

footpath around two boundaries of

the property

Fees of £ ..24.00..are enclosed, including fees for an Official Search.

Replies are requested to the following Enquiries contained in the 1982 Edition of form CON 29A ENGLAND AND WALES (EXCLUDING LONDON), subject to the headnotes and footnotes set out on that form:

Signed ....Smiths............................... (*Solicitors*) Dated ....1st May..................19 90......

PART I

All Enquiries

PART II

The following Enquiries (tick box(es) as required):

☐ **I** (Public paths, etc., map)	☐ **VIII** (Pipe-lines)
☐ **II** (Stopping up/diversion of roads etc.)	☐ **IX** (Registration of houses scheme)
☐ **III** (Advertisements)	☐ **X** (Noise)
☐ **IV** (Listed buildings)	☐ **XI** (Urban development area)
☐ **V** (Repairs notice/"minimum compensation")	☐ **XII** (Enterprise zone)
☐ **VI** (Completion notice)	☐ **XIII** (Improvement area)
☐ **VII** (National Parks etc. Act 1949, s. 87 Order)	*For the fees relating to Part II Enquiries, see overleaf*

NAME AND ADDRESS (IN BLOCK LETTERS) TO WHICH THIS FORM IS TO BE RETURNED
MESSRS SMITHS SOLICITORS 99 LONG ROW BLACKSVILLE, BROWNSHIRE

SOLICITORS' REFERENCE ...RC/1234

TELEPHONE NUMBER ....Jonesborough 56789

TELEX.................

Form LLC1. (*Local Land Charges Rules 1977 Schedule 1. Form C*)

**The duplicate of this form must also be completed:
a carbon copy will suffice**

For directions, notes and fees see overleaf

Insert name and address of registering authority in space below

> Jonesborough District Council
> 2 High Street
> Jonesborough
> Brownshire

Official Number_____
(*To be completed by the registering authority*)

Register of local land charges

Requisition for search and official certificate of search

---

fold

Requisition for search
(*A separate requisition must be made in respect of each parcel of land except as explained overleaf*)

An official search is required in *Part(s)*_____of [1]
the register of local land charges kept by the above-named
registering authority for subsisting registrations against the land
[defined in the attached plan and] [2] described below.

Description of land sufficient to enable it to be identified

> 72 Black Horse Lane, Jonesborough
> edged in red on the plan attached

Name and address to which certificate is to be sent

> MESSRS SMITHS
> SOLICITORS
> 99 LOW ROW
> BLACKSVILLE
> BROWNSHIRE

Signature of applicant (*or his solicitor*)

Smiths

Date

1st May 1990
Telephone number

Jonesborough 56789
Reference

_RC/1234_

Enclosure
Cheque/~~Money Order/Postal Order/Cash~~

Official certificate of search

It is hereby certified that the search requested above reveals
no subsisting registrations [3]

*or the*_____registrations described in the Schedule
hereto [3] up to and including the date of this certificate.

To be completed by
authorised officer

Signed ....

On behalf of ....
Date

---

1 Delete if inappropriate. Otherwise insert Part(s) in which
   search is required.

2 Delete if inappropriate. (A plan should be furnished
   in duplicate if it is desired that a copy should be returned.)

3 Delete inapplicable words. (The Parts of the Schedule should
   be securely attached to the certificate and the number of
   registrations disclosed should be inserted in the space provided.
   Only Parts which disclose subsisting registrations should be sent.)

4 Insert name of registering authority.

Application for an
Official Search
of the Index Map

HM Land Registry

Form **96**

FOR EXPLANATORY NOTES SEE OVERLEAF
Please complete in typescript or in BLACK BLOCK LETTERS all details within the thick black lines.
Use one application form for each parcel of land. (Note 1)

(Rule 3 Land Registration Rules 1990)

To   EDMUNDS   District Land Registry

1 DOWNHAM WAY
NEEDHAM

For official use only

Description		Date
Fees Debited £		Record of Fee paid

(Note 2)

I   R C Smith
of   Messrs Smiths
        99 Low Row
        Blacks ville
        Brownshire

(enter here name and address of person or firm making the application)

apply for an official search of the Index Map or General Map and Parcels Index, and the list of pending applications for first registration, in respect of the property referred to below and shown [edged in red] on the attached plan.
NOTE - Any attached plan must contain sufficient details of the surrounding roads and other features to enable the land to be identified satisfactorily on the Ordnance Map. However, a plan is normally unnecessary if the parcel of land can be identified by postal description. Nevertheless, the Chief Land Registrar reserves the right to ask for a plan to be supplied where he deems it necessary.

PAYMENT OF FEE (Note 4)

Please enter X in the appropriate box:-
☐ the Land Registry fee of £ [   ] accompanies this application,
or
☒ please debit the Credit Account mentioned below with the appropriate fee payable under the current Land Registration Fee Order.

FOR COMPLETION BY APPLICANTS WHO ARE CREDIT ACCOUNT HOLDERS

YOUR KEY NUMBER:-

YOUR REFERENCE:-

Signed   R C Smith
Date   1st May 1990
Telephone No.   0798 32323
Reference   RC/1234

- -

HM Land Registry   CERTIFICATE OF RESULT OF OFFICIAL SEARCH OF THE INDEX MAP   (Form 96 Result)

Property

Postal number or description	No 72
Name of road	Black Horse Lane
Name of locality	Jonesborough
Town	
Postcode	J07 1YP
District or London Borough	Edmunds
Administrative County	Brownshire
Ordnance Map Reference	(Note 3)
Known Title Number(s)	

Enter Name and Address
(to which the official certificate of result of search is to be sent.)

Reference

(Revised 4/90)

It is certified that the official search applied for has been made with the following result :- (Only the statements opposite the boxes marked X apply.)

☐ The land
is not registered. (Note 5)

☐ The land
is not affected by any caution against first registration or any priority notice.

☐ The land
is affected by a pending application for first registration under the following reference

☐ The land
is registered freehold under Title No

☐ The land
is registered leasehold under Title No

☐ The land
is affected by a rentcharge under Title No

☐ The land
is affected by a caution against first registration/ priority notice under Title No

Official stamp

Please enclose this result of search and any plan annexed thereto with any correspondence or application for first registration relating to the above property.

AGREEMENT
(Incorporating the Standard Conditions of Sale (First Edition))

Agreement date	:	1 June 1990
Seller	:	John Alan Smith of No. 72 Black Horse Lane, Jonesborough
Buyer	:	Frederick Brown and Ada Brown of 92 Bishops Street, Charlestown
Property (freehold/leasehold)	:	72 Black Horse Lane Jonesborough
Burdens on the Property	:	Restrictive Covenants contained in a deed of conveyancing dated 3 July 1953
Capacity in which the seller sells	:	Beneficial Owner
Completion date	:	10 July 1990
Contract rate	:	4% above the base rated charged by the Law Society's Bankers for the time being
~~Root of title~~/Title Number	:	AA 1234
Purchase price	:	£95,000.00
Deposit	:	£9,500.00
Amount payable for chattels	:	£1,000.00
Balance	:	£86,500.00

The Seller will sell and the Buyer will buy the Property for the Purchase Price.
The Agreement continues on the back page.

WARNING This is a formal document, designed to create legal rights and legal obligations. Take advice before using it.	**Signed**  Seller/Buyer

(Reproduced by permission of The Law Society and of The Solicitors' Law Stationery Society Limited.)

SPECIAL CONDITIONS

1. (a) This Agreement incorporates the Standard Conditions of Sale (First Edition). Where there is a conflict between those Conditions and this Agreement, this Agreement prevails.

(b) Where the context so admits terms used or defined in this Agreement have the same meaning when used in the Conditions.

2. The Property is sold subject to the Burdens on the Property and the Buyer will raise no requisitions on them.

3. The chattels on the Property and set out on any attached list are included in the sale.

4. All sums payable under this Agreement are exclusive of Value Added Tax.

Seller's Solicitors

Buyer's Solicitors

This form may be used as part of the Law Society's TransAction Scheme

Standard Conditions of Sale

Short description
of the property

re 72 Black Horse Lane,.............................
Jonesborough
Parties .....Smith..................................

to .Brown..

**These enquiries are copyright
and may not be reproduced**

Replies are requested to the following enquiries.

Smiths
....
Proposed purchaser's solicitors.

Date.......19th March.................1990

GENERAL ENQUIRIES

cyez
ENQUIRIES
BEFORE CONTRACT

In cases of property subject to a
tenancy, forms **Con 291** (general
business and residential tenancies)
or **Con 292** (agricultural tenancies)
should also be used.

**Please strike out enquiries
which are not applicable**

The replies are as follows.

Proposed vendor's solicitors.

Date.......1st April.....................1990

REPLIES

These replies, except in the case of any enquiry expressly requiring a reply
from the Vendor's solicitors, are given on behalf of the proposed Vendor
and without responsibility on the part of his solicitors their partners or
employees. They are believed to be correct but the accuracy is not
guaranteed and they do not obviate the need to make appropriate
searches, enquiries and inspections.

1. Boundaries
(A) To whom do all the boundary walls, fences, hedges and ditches
belong?

(B) If no definite indications exist, which has the Vendor maintained or
regarded as his responsibility?

Left hand boundary belongs to vendor

Not applicable

2. Disputes
(A) Is the Vendor aware of any past or current disputes regarding
boundaries, easements, covenants or other matters relating to the
property or its use?

(B) During the last three years, has the Vendor complained or had
cause to complain about the state and condition, or the manner of
use, of any adjoining or neighbouring property? If so, please give
particulars

No

No

3. Notices
Please give particulars of all notices relating to the property, or to
matters likely to affect its use or enjoyment, that the Vendor (or to his
knowledge, any predecessor in title) has given or received.

None received to the vendors knowledge

4. Guarantees etc.
(A) Please supply a copy of any of the following of which the
Purchaser is to have the benefit.
    agreement, covenant, guarantee, warranty, bond, certificate,
    indemnity and insurance policy.
relating to any of the following matters.
    the construction of the property, or any part of it, or of any
    building of which it forms part;
    any repair or replacement of, or treatment or improvement to the
    fabric of the property.
    the maintenance of any accessway.
    the construction costs of any road (including lighting, drainage
    and crossovers) to which the property fronts, and the charges for
    adopting any such road as maintainable at the public expense;
    a defective title;
    breach of any restrictive covenant

(B) (i) What defects or other matters have become apparent, or
    adverse claims have been made by third parties, which might give
    rise to a claim under any document mentioned in (A)?
    (ii) Has notice of such defect, matter or adverse claim been
    given? If so, please give particulars
    (iii) Please give particulars of all such claims already made,
    whether or not already settled.

A. The property has the benefit of
an N.H.B.C. certificate, a copy of which
is enclosed.

None

(Reproduced by permission of The Solicitors' Law Stationery Society Limited.)

5. Services

(A) Does the property have drainage, water, electricity and gas services? Which of them are connected to the mains?

(B) Is the water supply metered?

(C) Do any of the services (except where part of the mains) pass through or over property not included in the sale?

(D) If so, please give details of route and particulars of any easement, grant, exception, reservation, wayleave, licence or consent authorising this.

(E) Please supply a copy of any licence to abstract water and of any consent or licence relating to drainage, issued in respect of the property or the activities carried on there.

The property has the benefit of all mains services except gas

No

Not so far as the vendors are aware, but no warranty is given and the purchasers must inspect
D. As far as the vendors are aware this is not applicable.
D. None

6. Facilities

(A) Except in the case of public rights or where particulars have already been given, what rights are there for the use of the following facilities, whether enjoyed by the owner or occupier of the property, or over the property for the benefit of other property:
— Access for light and air;
— Access for pedestrians and vehicles;
— Emergency escape routes;
— Pipes and wires for services not dealt with in Enquiry 5.
— Access and facilities for repair, maintenance and replacement.
Please supply copies of any relevant documents.

There are no such facilities

(B) Has any person taken any action to stop (whether immediately or at some future time) the use of any facility? If so, please give particulars.

Not applicable

(C) In respect of maintenance, repair or replacement work on any land or fixtures affording any facility:
(i) What work has been done by the Vendor (or, to his knowledge, any predecessor in title), and when?
(ii) What work has the Vendor been called upon to do which has not yet been done?
(iii) What sums has the Vendor contributed to work done by others, and when? Is any demand for such sums still outstanding?
(iv) What sums has the Vendor called upon others to contribute, and when? Is any demand still outstanding?

Not applicable

7. Adverse Rights

(A) Is the Vendor aware of any rights or informal arrangements specifically affecting the property, other than any disclosed in the draft contract or immediately apparent on inspection, which are exercisable by virtue of an easement, grant, wayleave, licence, consent, agreement relating to an ancient monument or land near it, or otherwise or which are in the nature of public or common rights?

No

(B) (i) Please give the full names, and ages if under 18, of all persons in actual occupation of the property.

(ii) What legal or equitable interest in the property has each of those persons?

The vendor alone resides at the property

(C) Is the Vendor aware of any other overriding interests as defined by the Land Registration Act 1925, s. 70(1)?

No

8. Restrictions

(A) Have all restrictions affecting the property or its use been observed up to the date hereof? If not, please give details.

As far as the vendor is aware

(B) Where such restrictions have in the past required any person's consent or approval of plans, does the Vendor have written evidence of that consent or approval?

Not applicable

9. Planning etc.

(A) (i) When did the present use of the property commence?
(ii) Has this use been continuous since it commenced?

(B) During the four years immediately prior to receipt of these enquiries:
(i) Were any of the buildings on the property erected, or have any been altered or added to?
(ii) Have any other building, engineering, mining or other operations been carried out in, on, over or under the property?
(iii) Has any condition or limitation on any planning permission not been complied with?
If so, please give details.

(i) 19 80
(ii) Yes
B. During this period the vendor has erected a conservatory and added a garage to the property

(C) Please supply a copy of:
  (i) Any planning permission authorising or imposing conditions upon the present use of the property, and the erection or retention of the buildings now on it.
  (ii) Any bye-law approval or building regulation consent relating to those buildings.
  (iii) Any current fire certificate.

Copies of the planning permision of which the vendor is aware are enclosed. The vendor believes that all conditions have been complied with.

10. Fixtures, Fittings etc.

(A) Does the sale include all of the following items now on the property, and attached to or growing in it?

  Trees, shrubs, plants, flowers, and garden produce. Greenhouses, garden sheds and garden ornaments. Aerials. Fitted furniture and shelves. Electric switches, points and wall and ceiling fittings.

(B) What fixtures and fittings affixed to the property are not included in the sale?

(C) If the property has any fixed oil burning appliance, what arrangements are proposed for the sale to the purchaser on completion of any stock of oil?

The vendor proposes to remove four apple trees in the garden and the chandeliers in the dining room.

Jnly as abobe

There are no such appliances at this property

11. Outgoings

(A) (i) What is the rateable value of the property?
    (ii) Have any works been carried out at the property which might result in a revision of this?

(B) Does the hereditament, in which the property to be sold is included for rating purposes, also include any other property?

(C) What annual or periodic charges, other than general and water rates, affect the property or its occupier?

(i)   £383
(ii) Yes – as above

B. No

None

12. Completion

(A) How long after exchange of contracts will the Vendor be able to give vacant possession of the whole of the property?

(B) The Purchaser's solicitors wish to complete by adopting the Law Society's Code for Completion by Post (1984 edition). Do the Vendor's solicitors agree?

This will be agreed when contracts are exchanged

Yes

13. New Properties

(A) Will the Vendor pay all charges for construction and connection of the drainage system and the services?

(B) Are all the following included in the purchase price: fencing all boundaries, laying all paths and drives, and levelling and clearing the garden area? If not, please give particulars.

Not applicable.

ADDITIONAL ENQUIRIES

For Leasehold Enquiries and further Additional Enquiries see over

71

LEASEHOLD ENQUIRIES

I. General

(A) Is the lease under which the property is held a head lease or an underlease?

(B) Please state the names and addresses of the lessor, any superior lessors, their respective solicitors, and the receivers of the rent.

(C) Please supply copies of all licences granted by the lessor, other than licences to assign.

(D) What steps have been taken to obtain the lessor's consent to the proposed assignment? Please supply a copy of any licence granted.

II. Covenants

(A) Has the lessor complained of any breach of covenant?

(B) Has any obligation in the lease to paint or do any other work by or at a particular time been strictly fulfilled? If not, please give details.

(C) Has the Vendor had cause to complain of any breach of the lessor's covenants?

III. Service Charge

(A) Please give details of service charge payments for the last three years, with any supporting accounts or vouchers that the Vendor has.

(B) Has the Vendor, or to his knowledge any predecessor in title, exercised a statutory right to obtain information? If so, with what result?

IV. Insurance

(A) Who effected the insurance policy currently covering the property?

(B) Please give particulars: insurers' and any insurance brokers' name and address, policy number, insured's name(s), risks covered, for what amount, premium, and date to which the property is insured.

V. Reversionary Title

Is there with the title deeds a marked abstract or office copy of the freehold title and of any superior lease?

ADDITIONAL ENQUIRIES

Head lease

Button Ltd. registered office 10 Market Street, Bromesville. solicitors Jack and Co. 4 St. Matthews Stree, Francistown.
C. None.
D. The proposed assignees references are being considered by the lessors solicitors.
A. No
B. Yes
C. No

A. The receipts for the last 3 years are enclosed
B. No

A. The Lessor

B. A copy of the lessor'spolicy is enclosed

No

PROPERTY INFORMATION FORM

Property: 68 BLACK HORSE LANE JONESBOROUGH

Seller: A.A. BEE

Buyer: R.R. SEE

1   Boundaries

Questions	Replies
1.1 Who owns all the boundary walls, fences, hedges, ditches or other boundary features?	The Seller owns all such structures
1.2 Who accepts responsibility for repairing the above?	The Seller
1.3 If there is no definite indication, please state which boundary features have been maintained or repaired by the seller or those which the seller considers to be his responsibility.	N/A
1.4 Has the position of any boundary feature been altered during the last 20 years?	No

2   Disputes

2.1 Please give full details of any past or current disputes which in any way relate to the property, its use or any adjoining or neighbouring property or their use.	None to the seller's knowledge
2.2 Have there been any disputes relating to any covenants or any boundaries affecting the property?	Not to the seller's knowledge

3   Notices

3.1 Please give full details of all notices given or received that relate to the property, to its use or to its covenants or boundaries.	None to the seller's knowledge

This form comprises 4 pages. Please ensure you complete all sections on all pages.   Please turn over to next page.   TA1/1

(Reproduced by permission of The Law Society.)

3.2 Please give details of any notices given or
received relating to any adjoining or neighbouring
properties or its covenants or boundaries.

None to the seller's knowledge

3.3 Is the seller aware of any correspondence or
negotiations with any local or other authority
which might affect the property?

No

4 Guarantees

If the property has the benefit of any guarantees:

4.1 Please supply copies together with details or
specifications of work done.

There are none

4.2 Please indicate what claims (if any) have already
been made under the guarantee and with
what result.

N/A

4.3 If appropriate, have notices of assignment of
the guarantee been given in the past?

N/A

5 Services

5.1 Please give details of any services or conducting
media other than mains which pass under or over
any adjoining or neighbouring property.

To the extent these may exist the
sellers provides the usual
reciprocal arrangements

5.2 Please give details of any services or conducting
media other than mains which pass under or over
the property and serve any adjoining or
neighbouring property.

The seller does not know the
specific details

5.3 Please give full details of all legal rights enjoyed
to ensure the benefit of uninterrupted services.
e.g. easements, wayleaves, licences etc.

Only as disclosed by the office
copy entries

6 Facilities

6.1 With regard to the use of any joint facilities
(such as accessway or drainage), please supply full
details of all contributions made or requested
towards the repair, renewal, maintenance or use of
such facilities or any obligations for making such
contributions.

No such facilities

6.2 Who is responsible for the collection of the
contributions and for the renewal, repair or
maintenance of such facilities?

N/A

TA1/2

6.3   Please give details of sums paid or owing.

N/A

6.4   Please indicate whether the payments are of
a regular nature.

N/A

6.5   In order to repair or maintain this property or any
of its boundary features, has the seller found it
necessary to enter onto any adjoining or
neighbouring property?

Yes

If so, how has permission been obtained?

The title provides for this.

7   Adverse Rights

7.1   Please give full details of all overriding interests
affecting the property as defined by the Land
Registration Act 1925 Section 70(1).

None to the seller's knowledge

7.2   Is the seller aware of any rights or other
arrangements of either a formal or informal
nature which affect the property other than those
already disclosed in the draft contract? If so, full
details should be supplied.

No

8   Occupiers

8.1   Please provide the full names, and ages if under
18, of all persons who are in occupation of the
property.

There are none

8.2   (a) Do any of the people mentioned in 8.1 have
any legal or equitable interest in the property or
any rights of occupation?

N/A

(b) If so, please supply full details and indicate if
such person will sign the contract to confirm that
vacant possession will be given on the
contractual completion date.

N/A

9   Restrictions

9.1   If the property is subject to any restrictive
covenant or other restriction which requires
consent to be given for certain acts or plans,
please provide written evidence of any such
consent or approval.

N/A

9.2   Is the seller aware that any necessary consent was
not in fact obtained?

N/A

TA1/3

9.3 Does the seller know who has the benefit of such restrictive covenants? If so, please provide the name and address of the person or company having such benefit or the name and address of his or its solicitors.

N/A

10 Planning

10.1 Has the seller (or to his knowledge any previous owner) carried out any alterations or additions to the property during the last 4 years?

Yes

10.2 If so, did such alterations or additions require planning consent, building regulations or bye-law approval or listed building consent?

Copy building regulations consent herewith

11 Mechanics of Sale

11.1 (a) Is this sale dependent on the seller buying another property?

Yes

(b) If so, what stage have the negotiations reached?

Same as in this transaction

11.2 (a) Does the seller require a mortgage?

Yes

(b) If so, has an offer been received or a mortgage certificate obtained?

Yes

11.3 How soon after exchange of contracts does the seller anticipate being able to give vacant possession of the whole of the property?

2 weeks

12 Outgoings

12.1 Has the seller paid any annual or periodic charges other than water and general rates or community charge which affect the property?

No

Seller's Solicitor ___R C Smith___

Date: ___3.7.90___

Reminder

1. Copies of all relevant planning decisions, NHBC documents, guarantees and building regulation approvals should be supplied in addition to the information above together with the Fixtures, Fittings and Contents Form.
2. If the property is leasehold, also complete Additional Property Information Form.

TA1/4

THE LAW SOCIETY   This form is part of The Law Society's TransAction scheme. © The Law Society 1990.   2.90 F16192
The Law Society is the professional body for solicitors in England and Wales.
The Solicitors' Law Stationery Society Ltd., Oyez House, 27 Crimscott Street, London SE1 5TS.   oyez   5065053

TA1

FIXTURES FITTINGS AND CONTENTS

Address of the Property: 72 BLACK HORSE LANE

JONESBOROUGH

Place a tick in one of these two columns against every item.

Item		
TV Aerial		✓
Radio Aerial		✓
Immersion Heater	✓	
Hot Water Cylinder Jacket	✓	
Roof Insulation		✓
Wall Heaters		✓
Night Storage Heater		✓
Gas/Electric Fires	✓	
Light Fittings:		
Ceiling Lights	✓	
Wall Lights		✓
Lamp Shades	✓	
N.B If these are to be removed, it is assumed that they will be replaced by ceiling rose and socket, flex, bulb holder and bulb.		
Switches	✓	
Electric Points	✓	
Dimmer Switches		✓

(Reproduced by permission of The Law Society.)

Fluorescent Lighting		✓
Outside Lights		✓
Telephone Receivers:		
British Telecom	✓	
Own		
Burglar Alarm System		✓
Complete Central Heating System		✓
Extractor Fans	✓	
Doorbell/Chimes	✓	
Door Knocker	✓	
Door Furniture:		
Internal	✓	
External	✓	
Double Glazing		✓
Window Fitments		✓
Shutters/Grills		✓
Curtain Rails	✓	
Curtain Poles	✓	
Pelmets	✓	
Venetian Blinds		✓
Roller Blinds		✓
Curtains (Including Net Curtains):		
Lounge		✓
Dining Room		✓

TA5/2

	INCLUDED IN THE SALE	EXCLUDED FROM SALE PRESENT AT THE PROPERTY
Kitchen		✓
Bathroom		✓
Bedroom 1		✓
Bedroom 2		✓
Bedroom 3		✓
Bedroom 4		✓
Other Rooms (state which)		
1		✓
2		✓
3		✓
Carpets and other Floor Covering:		
Lounge	✓	
Dining Room	✓	
Kitchen		✓
Hall, Stairs and Landing	✓	
Bathroom		✓
Bedroom 1	✓	
Bedroom 2	✓	
Bedroom 3	✓	
Bedroom 4	✓	
Other Rooms (state which)		
1		✓

TA5/3

2		✓
3		✓
Storage Units in Kitchen		✓
Kitchen Fitments:		
Fitted Cupboards and Shelves	✓	
Refrigerator/ Fridge-Freezer		✓
Oven	✓	
Extractor Hood	✓	
Hob		✓
Cutlery Rack		✓
Spice Rack		✓
Other (state which)		
1		—
2		—
3		—
Kitchen Furniture:		
Washing Machine		✓
Dishwasher		✓
Tumble-Drier		✓
Cooker	✓	
Other (state which)		
1		✓

TA5/4

	INCLUDED IN THE SALE	FITTED BUT REMOVABLE OR NONE AT THE PROPERTY
2		✓
3		✓
Bathroom Fitments:		
Cabinet		✓
Towel Rails	✓	
Soap and Tooth-brush Holders		✓
Toilet Roll Holders	✓	
Fitted Shelves/ Cupboards		✓
Other Sanitary Fittings		✓
Shower		✓
Shower Fittings		✓
Shower Curtain		✓
Bedroom Fittings:		
Shelves		✓
Fitted Wardrobes		✓
Fitted Cupboards		✓
Fitted Shelving/ Cupboards		✓
Fitted Units		✓
Wall Mirrors	✓	
Picture Hooks	✓	✓
Plant Holders		✓
Clothes Line		✓
Rotary Line	✓	

Please turn over to next page.   TA5/5

Garden Shed	✓	
Greenhouse		✓
Garden Ornaments		✓
Trees, Plants and Shrubs	✓	
Garden Produce		✓
Stock of Oil/Solid Fuel/Propane Gas		✓
Water Butts		✓
Dustbins	✓	
Other		

TOTAL PRICE AGREED: £ 10,000

Signed Seller(s)   J. a. Smith

 THE LAW SOCIETY   This form is part of The Law Society's TransAction scheme. © The Law Society 1990.
The Law Society is the professional body for solicitors in England and Wales.

TA5/6

Form K15   Land Charges Act 1972   **Payment of fee**

APPLICATION FOR AN OFFICIAL SEARCH

NOT APPLICABLE TO REGISTERED LAND

Application is hereby made for an official search in the index to the registers kept pursuant to the Land Charges Act 1972 for any subsisting entries in respect of the under-mentioned particulars.

Insert a cross (X) in this box if the fee is to be paid through a credit account (see note 3 overleaf)   [X]

IMPORTANT: **Please read the notes overleaf before completing this form**

For Official Use only			NAMES TO BE SEARCHED (Please use block letters and see note 4 overleaf)		PERIOD OF YEARS (see note 5 overleaf)	
STX					From	To
		Forename(s)	JOHN ALAN		1935	1975
		SURNAME	SMITH			
		Forename(s)	FREDA MARGARET		1935	1975
		SURNAME	SMITH			
		Forename(s)	JOHNSON LIMITED		1985	1988
		SURNAME				
		Forename(s)				
		SURNAME				
		Forename(s)				
		SURNAME				
		Forename(s)				
		SURNAME				

COUNTY (see note 6 overleaf)	SHARPSVILLE
FORMER COUNTY	BROWNVILLE
DESCRIPTION OF LAND (see note 7 overleaf)	
FORMER DESCRIPTION	

Particulars of Applicant (see notes 8, 9 and 10 overleaf)		[Name and address for despatch of certificate] (Leave blank if certificate is to be returned to applicant's address)
KEY NUMBER	Name and address	
12345	MESSRS SMITHS 99 LOW ROW BLACKSVILLE BROWNSHIRE	

Applicant's reference: R C / 1 2 3 4	Date 16.6.90	FOR OFFICIAL USE ONLY

Short description of the property re ....72 Black Horse Lane,........ Jonesborough	———— oyez ————

REQUISITIONS

Parties ....Smith............

ON TITLE

to ....Brown........

(For use where Enquiries before Contract have already been answered)

These requisitions are copyright and may not be reproduced

Please strike out any requisitions not applicable.

---

1. PREVIOUS ENQUIRIES

If the enquiries before contract replied to on behalf of the Vendor were repeated herein, would the replies now be the same as those previously given? If not, please give full particulars of any variation.

Yes. Subject is varied if at all by subsequent correspondence between us.

---

2. OUTGOINGS AND APPORTIONMENTS

(A) On completion the Vendor must produce receipts for the last payments of outgoings, of which either he claims reimbursement of an advance payment or arrears could be recovered from the Purchaser.

(B) (i) In the case of a leasehold property or property subject to a legal rentcharge, the receipt for rent due on the last rent day before the day of completion, as well as the receipt for the last fire insurance premium, must be produced on completion.

(ii) Does the former receipt contain any reference to a breach of any of the covenants and conditions contained in the lease or grant?

(C) Please send a completion statement.

Noted. The vendor confirms that all outgoings will be discharged to the completion date.

(i) Noted

(ii) No

C. Herewith

---

3. TITLE DEEDS

A. *Unregistered land*

(i) Which abstracted documents of title will be delivered to the Purchaser on completion?

(ii) Who will give to the Purchaser the statutory acknowledgment and undertaking for the production and safe custody of those not handed over?

(iii) Why will any documents not handed over be retained?

B. *Registered land*

(i) When was the land or charge certificate last officially examined with the register?

(ii) If the Land Registry has approved an estate lay-out plan for use with official searches of part of the land in the title, on what date was it approved?

(iii) If the Vendor's land certificate is on deposit at the Land Registry, what is the deposit number?

(i) 9.6.90

(ii) N/A

(iii) N/A

---

4. MORTGAGES

(A) All subsisting mortgages must be discharged on or before completion.

(B) In respect of each subsisting mortgage or charge:

(i) Will a vacating receipt, discharge of registered charge or consent to dealing, entitling the Purchaser to take the property freed from it, be handed over on completion?

(ii) If not, will the Vendor's solicitor give a written undertaking on completion to hand one over later?

(iii) If an undertaking is proposed, what are the suggested terms of it?

Noted

Please accept this as our undertaking to discharge the subsisting mortgage in favour of the Big Town Building Society upon completion and to remit the duly sealed form 53 to you as soon as it is returned to us by the Big Town Building Society.

(Reproduced by permission of The Solicitors' Law Stationery Society Limited.)

5. POSSESSION

(A) (i) Vacant possession of the whole of the property must be given on completion.

The contract provides for this

(ii) Has every person in occupation of all or any part of the property agreed to vacate on or before completion?

Yes

(iii) What arrangements will be made to deliver the keys to the Purchaser?

These will be available for collection from the estate agents

Or

(B) The Vendor must on completion hand over written authorities for future rents to be paid to the Purchaser or his agents.

N/A

6. NOTICES

Please give the name and address of any solicitor, residential tenant or other person to whom notice of any dealing with the property must be given.

Jack and Co., 4 St. Matthew Street, Francistown.

7. COMPLETION ARRANGEMENTS

Please answer any of the following requisitions against which X has been placed in the box.

[X] (A) Where will completion take place?

At our office

[ ] (B) We should like to remit the completion monies direct to your bank account. If you agree, please give the name and branch of your bank, its sorting code number, and the title and number of the account to be credited.

Downtown Bank PLC, sorting code. 99.99.99

Smiths Client account no. 1234567

[ ] (C) We should like to remit the completion monies by Speedsend. If you agree, please give the address of the most convenient Trustee Savings Bank branch and state whether you maintain an account there.

There are no branches of this bank in the vicinity of our office.

[ ] (D) In whose favour and for what amounts will banker's drafts be required on completion?

One for the balance due on the enclosed completion statement.

The deeds and documents of title remain to be examined and the right is reserved to make further requisitions which may arise on such examination, the replies to the above, the usual searches and enquiries before completion, or otherwise.

Noted

Note.—The Requisitions founded on the Abstract of Title or Contract must, of course, be added to the above.

DATED   *Smiths*   198

DATED   16th June   1990

Purchaser's Solicitor.   *Vendor's Solicitor.*

oyez The Solicitors' Law Stationery Society plc, Oyez House, 27 Crimscott Street, London SE1 5TS   *revised 2 84* 2.86 B'HAM

5032056

Conveyancing 28B

85

Application for
Office Copies of
register and plan only

HM Land Registry

A44

| EDMUNDS | District Land Registry |
| 1 Downham Way |
| Needham |

Application for office copies of Specified Deeds must be made on form A44A.

For official use only

(1) Please complete the white boxes on this form in typescript or BLOCK LETTERS. No covering letter is necessary and no fee is payable.

(2) Enter address, including any postcode, (or short description) of property.

(3) Enter full name(s) of registered proprietor(s)

Title number—A separate form must be used for each title number | AA 1234

Property[2] 72 BLACK HORSE LANE
JONESBOROUGH

County | BROWNSHIRE

Proprietor(s)[3]
JOHN ALAN SMITH

Application

I/We hereby apply for the office copies specifed below

(4) Enter name and address of person or firm making application.

[4] MESSRS SMITHS

of 99 LOW ROAD BLACKSVILLE BROWNSHIRE

(5) Please state in the appropriate box(es) the number of copies required.

[5] Register entries | X

[5] Title plan | X

For official use only

(6) Form 102 is a simpler and quicker alternative to obtaining an office copy of a large title plan for the purpose of a sale or other transaction affecting only a part of the land in a registered title.

[5] [6] Form 102

(7) Form 102 applications only. Please ✓ appropriate box.

[7] Has an estate plan been approved? Yes ☐

No ☐

If YES, enter plot no(s)

Approved by

Date

Despatched by

Date

(8) Where no estate plan has been approved a plan must be lodged in duplicate. It should be drawn to a suitable scale (generally not less than 1/2500) and must show by suitable markings the extent of the land affected and, where necessary, figured measurements to fix the position of the land by tying it to existing physical features depicted by firm black lines on the plan of the registered title.

[8] If NO, the certificate to be issued in respect of the land shown _____ on the attached plan.

The authority panel overleaf must be completed.

Please enter your name and address in the return slip overleaf.

Continued

Authority

(9) Enter ✓ in the appropriate box

I/We declare that:

A   Solicitor(s)/licensed conveyancer(s)/recognised body acting

or

B   No solicitor(s)/licensed conveyancer(s)/recognised body acting

(9)

☐ I/We hold the duly signed written authority of (or of the solicitor(s)/licensed conveyancer(s)/recognised body for) the registered proprietor(s) named overleaf.

☐ I/We act for the registered proprietor(s) named overleaf

☐ I am/We are the registered proprietor(s) of the title number set out overleaf.

☐ The duly signed written authority of (or of the solicitor(s)/licensed conveyancer(s)/recognised body for) the registered proprietor(s) to inspect the register of the title number set out overleaf accompanies this application.

Signed _Smiths_   Date _25.5.90_

Daytime telephone no. _56789_   Ref _RC/1234_

(10) Enter ✓ in the appropriate box

(10)

☐ If there is an application for registration pending against the title— do you want **office copies back dated** to the day prior to the receipt of that application?

or

☐ do you want **office copies on completion** of that application? **Important—Please read note (c) below**

Notes for guidance of applicants

(a) Full information on all aspects of applications for office copies is set out in Practice Leaflet No. 13 which is obtainable free from any district land registry.

(b) The application should be sent to the district land registry serving the area in which the land is situated. A list of addresses of the district land registries is set out in Explanatory Leaflet No. 9 which is obtainable free from any land registry office.

(c) If there is a pending application and you are applying for an office copy in connection with a further transaction it is possible for negotiations to proceed on the strength of a back-dated office copy of the register which can be brought up-to-date in effect by making a non-priority official search in form 94C in which the

date of that office copy is entered as the date for the commencement of the search. The certificate of result of search will reveal details of the pending application for registration and will state whether or not it has yet been approved for entry on the register.

If negotiations proceed on this basis, and assuming that your prospective transaction is a transfer, lease or charge, the normal search in form 94A or 94B can be made as usual immediately before the completion of the transaction.

If a back dated office copy is not required, as indicated above, your application for office copies will be returned to you. You will be informed when the pending application has been completed and invited to re-apply for office copies at that time.

Printed in the United Kingdom for Her Majesty's Stationery Office
Dd 291037 C500 3/89   45p each   25 for £4   100 for £14 (exclusive of tax)   ISBN 0 11 390322 7

Reference ____ _RC/1234_ ____

MESSRS SMITHS
SOLICITORS
99 LOW ROW
BLACKS VILLE
BROWNSHIRE

Please enter above using BLOCK LETTERS the name, address and reference to whom the office copies are to be sent.

Application by **Purchaser** **for Official Search** with **priority in respect of the** **whole of the land in a title**	**HM Land Registry**	**Form 94A** Duplicate (Land Registration (Official Searches) Rules 1988) For an official search of part of the land in a title use form 94B.
		For official use

EDMUNDS _____ District Land Registry

1 Downham Way
Needham

County and district (or London Borough) (Enter opposite)	Jonesborough, Brownshire
Title number (Enter opposite)	AA 1234
Full name(s) of the registered proprietor(s) (Enter opposite)	John Alan Smith
Date on which an office copy of the subsisting entries in the register was issued or the last date on which the land or charge certificate was officially examined with the register.	14th January 1981
Full name(s) of the applicants (i.e. purchaser(s) lessee(s) or charge(s)) (Enter opposite)	Big Town Building Society
I/We certify that the applicant(s) intend(s) to: (Enter X in the appropriate box opposite)	X P purchase L take a lease of X C lend money on the security of a registered charge on the whole of the land in the above title
Address, including any postcode, or short description of property (Enter opposite)	72 Black Horse Lane Jonesborough J07 1YP

A. Where solicitor(s)/licensed conveyancer(s)/ recognised body is/are acting for the applicant(s) I/We certify that I/we hold the duly signed written authority of [or of the solicitor(s)/licensed conveyancer(s)/recognised body for] the above-mentioned registered proprietor(s) to inspect the register of the above title. or that I/we also act for the registered proprietor(s).	In either case indicate this by entering X in the box below. X A	**B.** Where solicitor(s)/licensed conveyancer(s) recognised body is/are not acting for the applicant(s) The duly signed written authority of [or of the solicitor(s) licensed conveyancer(s) recognised body for] the registered proprietor(s) to inspect the register of the above title accompanies this application.	Indicate this by entering X in the box below. B

Key Number 12345	Complete this panel using BLOCK LETTERS and insert the name and address to which the official certificate of result of search is to be sent.
MESSRS SMITHS 99 LOW ROW BLACKSVILLE BROWNSHIRE	

Application is made to ascertain whether any adverse entry has been made in the register or daylist since the date shown above.

Signed   Smiths

Date   16th June 1990

Reference	RC/ 1234	Telephone No. 0789 32323

Transfer of Whole to Joint Proprietors [1]

HM Land Registry

Form 19(JP)

(Rules 98 or 115, Land Registration Rules, 1925)

Stamp pursuant to section 28 of the Finance Act 1931 to be impressed here.

When the transfer attracts Inland Revenue Duty, the stamps should be impressed here before lodging the transfer for registration.

[1] *For a transfer to a sole proprietor use printed form 19.*

County and district (or London borough)

Title number(s) AA 1234

Property 72 Black Horse Lane, Jonesborough

Date 10 July 19 90 In consideration of ninety-five thousand

[2] *Delete the words in italics if not required.*

pounds (£ 95,000.00) *the receipt of which is hereby acknowledged* (²)

[3] *In BLOCK LETTERS enter the full name(s), postal address(es) (including postcode) and occupation(s) of the proprietor(s) of the land.*

I/We (³) JOHN ALAN SMITH

72 BLACK HORSE LANE

JONESBOROUGH JO7 1YP

[4] *If desired or otherwise as the case may be (see rules 76 and 77).*

as beneficial owner(s) hereby transfer to (⁴)

[5] *In BLOCK LETTERS enter the full name(s), postal address(es) (including postcode) and occupation(s) of the transferee(s) for entry in the register.*

(⁵) FREDERICK BROWN AND ADA BROWN
92 BISHOPS STREET
CHARLESTOWN

[6] *Enter any special clause here.*

the land comprised in the title(s) above mentioned (⁶) (⁷)

[7] *A transfer for charitable purposes should follow form 36 in the schedule to the Land Registration Rules, 1925 (see rules 121 and 122).*

To be held by the transferees as beneficial joint tenants.

(continued overleaf)

(Reproduced by permission of The Solicitors' Law Stationery Society Limited.)

(8) Delete the inappropriate alternative.

The transferees declare that the survivor of them (*) $\frac{can}{cannot}$ give a valid receipt for capital money arising on a disposition of the land.

(9) If a certificate of value for the purposes of the Stamp Act 1891 and amending Acts is not required delete this paragraph.

(*) ~~It is hereby certified that the transaction hereby effected does not form part of a larger transaction or series of transactions in respect of which the amount or value or aggregate amount or value of the consideration exceeds £~~

(10) This transfer must be executed by the transferee(s) as well as the transferor(s).

(10) Signed, sealed and delivered by the said
JOHN ALAN SMITH

Seal

in the presence of

Name   Signature of witness

Address

Occupation

(10) Signed, sealed and delivered by the said
FREDERICK BROWN

Seal

in the presence of

Name   Signature of witness

Address

Occupation

(10) Signed, sealed and delivered by the said
ADA BROWN

Seal

in the presence of

Name   Signature of witness

Address

Occupation

(10) Signed, sealed and delivered by the said

Seal

in the presence of

Name   Signature of witness

Address

Occupation

oyez The Solicitors' Law Stationery Society plc, 24 Gray's Inn Road, London WC1X 8HR   1988 Edition (Revised 7.88)
7.88 F8088
5061122
• • •

Discharge of registered charge

of which a company or corporation, including a building society, is the registered proprietor(¹)(²)

HM Land Registry

Form 53(Co.)

(Rule 151, Land Registration Rules, 1925)

(1) No Land Registry fee is payable.

(2) The charge certificate must accompany this application.

Title number(s) .... AA1234 ....

Property .... 72 Black Horse Lane, Jonesborough ....

(3) In BLOCK LETTERS, enter full name and address of the registered proprietor of the charge.

Date .... 15th December 1990 .... (³) Big Town Building Society
1 Upper Orwell Street, Tonbridge

hereby admits that the charge dated the 15th .... of ..December .... 19 ..80

and registered on the .... 14th .. of .... January .... 19 81 of which

(4) Cross out the words in brackets if discharge is of the whole of the charge. If a discharge of part of the money only is intended insert "to the extent of £ ...."

(5) A plan is not required where the part discharged is already defined on the official title plan by colour or number reference and such particulars are entered in the discharge. A discharge by reference to the plot number(s) on an estate layout plan is not acceptable. In all other cases a plan must be supplied based on the official title plan, where necessary including sufficient figured dimensions to identify the extent of the land discharged and to fix its position by tying it to those physical features shown by firm black lines on the official title plan. This plan must be properly sealed by the chargee and securely attached to this form.

(6) These words are required when the sealing is by a building society.

it is proprietor has been discharged (⁴) [~~as to the land shown and edged with red on the~~

~~accompanying plan (⁵) sealed by the said proprietor (⁶) being part of the land comprised in the~~

~~title(s) above referred to~~].

The common seal of .... THE Big Town Building Society ....

was hereunto affixed (⁶) by order of the board of directors

in the presence of

(7) Or other officers authorised by the statute, charter, articles of association, etc.

.... (⁷) *Director*

.... (⁷) *Secretary*

(⁶) By authority of the board of directors.

9.86 B'HAM
5061287

91

Inland Revenue

PARTICULARS OF INSTRUMENTS TRANSFERRING OR LEASING LAND

SECTION 28 FINANCE ACT 1931
as amended by the Land Commission Act, 1967
and Section 89 Finance Act 1985

FOR OFFICIAL USE	
VO No.	....
PD No.	....
ANALYSIS CODE	....
DESC.	....
GV/NAV	....
DW. CODE.	....
	....
RETURN	....
O.S. No.	....
OTHER	....

1. **Description of Instrument**
   Conveyance

2. **Date of Instrument**
   10 July 1990

3. **Name and Address of Transferor or Lessor:** *(Block Letters)*
   JOHN ALAN SMITH
   72 BLACK HORSE LANE
   JONESBOROUGH

4. **Name and Address of Transferee or Lessee:** *(Block Letters)*
   FREDERICK BROWN AND ADA BROWN
   92 BISHOPS STREET
   CHARLESTOWN

5. Situation of the Land. Sufficient information must be given to enable the land to be identified accurately, e.g., by including any dimensions stated in the instrument and by attaching a plan to this form or by describing the boundaries in full. For premises the full postal address including the post code is required. Please indicate whether a plan is provided in the appropriate box.

   72 Black Horse Lane
   Jonesborough
   J07 1YP

   Plan attached to this form   Yes ☐

   Plan attached   No ☐

COUNTY. Brownshire .... RATING AUTHORITY. ....

6. Estate or Interest Transferred. Where the transaction is the assignment or grant of a lease, or the transfer of a fee simple subject to a lease, the terms of the lease, the date of commencement of the term and the rent reserved must be stated.

   Fee simple

7. Consideration £95,000 State separately:

   (a) any capital payment, with the date when due if otherwise than on execution of the instrument:

   (b) any debt released, covenanted to be paid or to which the transaction is made subject:

   (c) any periodical payment (including any charge) covenanted to be paid:

   (d) any terms surrendered:

   (e) any land exchanged:

   (f) any other thing representing money or money's worth:

8. Any Minerals, Mineral Rights, Sporting Rights, Timber or Easements reserved: (on a separate sheet if necessary).

9. Any Restrictions, Covenants or Conditions affecting the value of the estate or interest transferred or granted: (on a separate sheet if necessary).

10. Signature of Transferee or Lessee or person on his behalf:

    Smiths   Date 15·6·90

13. **Name and Address of Transferor's or Lessor's Solicitor:** *(Block Letters)*
    MESSRS SMITHS
    SOLICITORS
    99 LOW ROW
    BLACKSVILLE, BROWNSHIRE

    STAMPS L(A) 451

12. **Name and Address of Signatory if other than Transferee or Lessee:** *(Block Letters)*
    MESSRS BROWN
    93 SHORT ROW
    WHITES VILLE
    CRFAMSHIRE

    Printed in the UK for HMSO
    Dd 813/960 C25000 11-88 8P12474

Application by
**Solicitors for
first registration of
freehold land.**

HM Land Registry

Form 1B

Please complete the white boxes on
pages 1, 2 and 3 in typescript or
BLOCK CAPITALS.

Code	Received stamp	Ack'd by
		A13 ☐
		Postcard ☐
		Initials
New title number	Record of fees paid	Date

Class of title applied for	
Amend if possessory title only is required	**Absolute**

1 Details of property
Enter the local authority name and
administrative County.

If there is no postal address, give a
short description of the land to be
registered (e.g. "Land on the south
west side of Rye Road").

1

District or London Borough	County
EDMUNDS DISTRICT	SHARPESHIRE

Postal number or description and road name

72 Black Horse Lane

Jonesborough

Town or place	Post code
	J07 1YP

2 Fees
Make sure you have enclosed the
correct fee; refer to the current Land
Registration Fee Order.

Cheques and postal orders should
be crossed and made payable to
"HM Land Registry".

No fee is payable for any mortgage
by the applicant lodged with this
application.

2

	Value £	Fee Scale	Fees paid £	Particulars of over under payments
Land and buildings	95,000		160	
Other fees				
		Total	160	

3 Applicants
Enter the full name(s), address(es)
in the United Kingdom (including
postcode), and descriptions of the
applicants e.g. "IAN HENRY,
Baker, and MAY HENRY, his wife,
both of 29 RYE ROAD, WARE,
HERTS WD3 4TQ."

NB The address(es) given here will
be entered on the register as the
proprietor's address for service of
notices etc.. If the applicant is a
company its registration number will
be entered on the register of title if
given here.

3

FREDERICK BROWN AND ADA BROWN
92 BISHOPS STREET
CHARLESTOWN

(Co. Regn. No.)

4 Deed inducing registration
Enter the date of the deed by which
the applicant acquired the property.

4 | Conveyance Transfer dated | 10.7.90 |

5 Person or firm lodging the application
Enter the name and address
(including postcode) of the person
or firm making the application to
whom any requisitions should be
sent and to whom all documents
(including Land or Charge
Certificates) will be issued unless
any special directions are given
in Panel 6.

5

Key No. (if any)	Requisitions to be sent to and documents returned to	S. Code
AA 1234		
MESSRS SMITHS SOLICITORS 99 LOW ROW BLACKSVILLE, BROWNSHIRE		

Reference	Telephone No.
RC/1234	0798 32323

6 Special directions
Specific request to the Land Registry
to issue document(s) to a person or
firm other than as mentioned in
Panel 5.

6 | Description of document and addressee |

NONE

Please turn to page 2

Page 1

7 Status of applicant
Put an X in box A, B or C. or specify at D the capacity in which the land is held e.g. "as trustees for sale upon the trusts of ...." "as personal representatives" "as tenant(s) for life".

7

The applicant(s)

A ☐ is the sole beneficial owner of the land.

B ☒ are joint owners holding the land for themselves as beneficial joint tenants.

C ☐ are joint owners holding the land for themselves as tenants in common.

D hold the land as ....

8 Corporate applicants
If the applicant is a corporate body evidence of its incorporation and powers is required. If any part of the certificate in this panel is not applicable delete and/or amend it as necessary and lodge a certified copy of the memorandum and articles of association or other appropriate evidence. If the applicant is not a corporate body this panel will be ignored by the Land Registry and the certificate need not be deleted.

8

a The applicant is a company trading for profit incorporated in England and Wales or Scotland under the Companies Acts.

b By its memorandum and articles of association it has power to hold, sell, mortgage, lease or otherwise deal with the land.

c Any charges made by the applicant have been registered with the Registrar of Companies and the certificates of registration are enclosed.

d Particulars are given in Panel 12 below of any floating charges created by the applicant on its assets.

e We are not aware of any petition or resolution for the winding up of the applicant.

9 Certificate of Title
If any part of this certificate cannot be given it should be amended. The position should be explained particularly where, due to a lapse of time or other reason, the practitioner who carried out the original investigation is not giving this certificate.

9

a We acted for the applicant on the purchase inducing this registration.

b The title has been investigated in the usual way and all necessary searches have been made.

c We believe that the applicant is, and has been since the date of the acquisition, in undisputed possession of the land or in receipt of the rents and profits thereof. We are not aware of any question or doubt affecting the title or of any claim to possession of the land adverse to the interest of the applicant.

d We are enclosing with this application all relevant deeds and documents which the applicant is able to produce. All abstracts of title and copy deeds have been verified and so marked.

e The land is subject only to matters mentioned in the conveyance to the applicant or in Panel 12 below.

f We certify that the information required has been supplied and is correct and we apply for the registration of the applicant as proprietor of the land.

10 Land Charges
If any entries disclosed in certificates of search in the Land Charges Department affect the land, enter here the official reference numbers of those entries and the dates of the deeds or other documents to which the entries refer.

10

Official reference number	Date of Deed

11 Merger:
This-panel should be completed only if merger of a lease is applied for. If that lease is registered lodge the Land/Charge Certificate. If the lease was also subject to an underlease, amend this panel accordingly and lodge the counterpart-underlease.

11

We apply that no note be made on the register of the lease

dated ....

which has been determined by merger.

We are not aware of any sub-lease or other incumbrance affecting the said lease

12 Incumbrances
Enter all incumbrances which
affect the title but which are not
mentioned in the deed inducing
registration. In particular, details
should be given of any charges,
estate contracts, leases, covenants,
and other matters entered into by
the applicant(s).
If there are none please enter
'NONE' opposite.

12

Legal charge dated 10.7.90 in favour of the Big Town
Building Society, 1 Upper Orwell Street, Tonbridge

13 Reminders

13

- Have you enclosed all relevant deeds and documents in the possession of the applicant(s), including searches, contracts, enquiries, requisitions and opinions of counsel? ☐
- Is the copy of the conveyance to the applicant(s) (and of any mortgage or charge to be registered) certified by a solicitor or in the name of the firm to be a true copy? ☐
- Have all dates and details been put in charges or mortgages? ☐
- Have you prepared a list in triplicate of all documents being delivered? ☐
- Have you enclosed Inland Revenue form L(A)451 duly completed (if appropriate)? ☐
- Have you enclosed a cheque for the appropriate amount? ☐

14 Signature

14

Signature of solicitors to the applicant	Date
Smiths	29.7.90

Page 3

95

Application to register **dealings with the whole of titles**	**HM Land Registry**		**Form A4**

Code	Received stamp	Ackd. by
		Postcard ☐
		Chargee Postcard ☐
Application number		Initials
		Date
	Record of fees paid.	
Enter District or London Borough		

Please complete the white boxes on page 1, 4 and 2 in typescript or **BLOCK CAPITALS.**

1 Title numbers
Enter title number(s) in this panel. If there are more than five, attach a list in alpha-numeric order e.g. 6342, AV4613, AV7542, BD1567 etc.

1

Title numbers	Pending application numbers
AA 1234	

2 Fees
Make sure you have enclosed the correct fee; refer to the current Land Registration Fee Order. Cheques and postal orders should be made payable to "HM Land Registry." Fees are payable on delivery of the application.

2

Nature of applications in priority order	Value £	Fee scale para or abatement	Fees paid £	Particulars of over/under payment
Form 53	nil		nil	
Transfer	95,000		160	
Mortgage			nil	
		Total	160	

3 Documents lodged
Treat each original and copy as a separate item.

3

List of all documents lodged	
Charge certificate	Mortgage
Form 53	Certified copy mortgage
Transfer	

4 Person or firm lodging application.
Name and address (including postcode) of person or firm lodging this application to whom any requisitions will be sent and to whom documents (including land or charge certificate) will be returned unless special directions are given in panel 5.

4

Key No. (if any)	Requisitions to be sent to and documents returned to	Type
	MESSRS JACK & CO	S.Code
	4 ST MATTHEW STREET	
	FRANCISTOWN	
Reference	Telephone No.	

5 Special directions
Special request to the Land Registry to issue a document to a person or firm not mentioned in panel 4.

5

Description of document and addressee
NOT APPLICABLE

Please turn to page 4 and complete panels 6 and 7.

Page 1

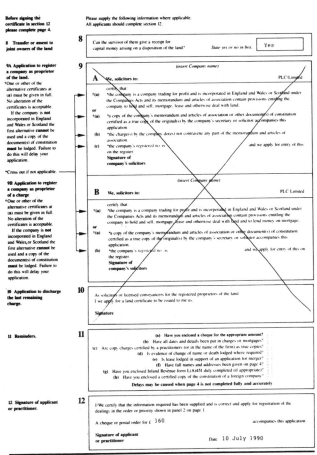

Before signing the
certificate in section 12
please complete page 4.

Please supply the following information where applicable.
All applicants should complete section 12.

**8 Transfer or assent to
joint owners of the land**

8   Can the survivor of them give a receipt for
capital money arising on a disposition of the land?   *State yes or no in box.*   Yes

**9A Application to register
a company as proprietor
of the land.**
†One or other of the
alternative certificates at
(a) must be given in full.
No alteration of the
certificates is acceptable.
   If the company is **not**
incorporated in England
and Wales or Scotland the
first alternative **cannot** be
used and a copy of the
document(s) of constitution
must be lodged. Failure to
do this will delay your
application.

*Cross out if not applicable.

**9B Application to register
a company as proprietor
of a charge**
†One or other of the
alternative certificates at
(a) must be given in full.
No alteration of the
certificates is acceptable.
   If the company is **not**
incorporated in England
and Wales, or Scotland the
first alternative **cannot** be
used and a copy of the
document(s) of constitution
must be lodged. Failure to
do this will delay your
application.

**10 Application to discharge
the last remaining
charge.**

11 Reminders.

**12 Signature of applicant
or practitioner.**

9   *(insert Company name)*

A   We, solicitors to: PLC/Limited
   certify that
†(a) *the company is a company trading for profit and is incorporated in England and Wales or Scotland under
   the Companies Acts and its memorandum and articles of association contain provisions entitling the
   company to hold and sell, mortgage, lease and otherwise deal with land.
or
†(a) *a copy of the company's memorandum and articles of association or other document(s) of constitution
   certified as a true copy of the originals(s) by the company's secretary or solicitor accompanies this
   application.
(b) *the charge(s) by the company does(t) not contravene any part of the memorandum and articles of
   association.
(c) *the company's registered no. is   and we apply for entry of this
   on the register
   Signature of
   company's solicitors

   (insert Company name)

B   We, solicitors to: PLC Limited
   certify that
†(a) *the company is a company trading for profit and is incorporated in England and Wales or Scotland under
   the Companies Acts and its memorandum and articles of association contain provisions entitling the
   company to hold and sell, mortgage, lease and otherwise deal with land and to lend money on mortgage.
or
†(a) *a copy of the company's memorandum and articles of association or other document(s) of constitution
   certified as a true copy of the originals(s) by the company's secretary or solicitor accompanies this
   application.
(b) *the company's registered no. is   and we apply for entry of this on
   the register.
   Signature of
   company's solicitors

10   As solicitors or licensed conveyancers for the registered proprietors of the land
   I/we apply for a land certificate to be issued to me us.
   Signature

11   (a)   Have you enclosed a cheque for the appropriate amount?
         (b)   Have all dates and details been put in charges or mortgages?
   (c)   Are copy charges certified by a practitioners (or in the name of the firm) as true copies?
         (d)   Is evidence of change of name or death lodged where required?
         (e)   Is lease lodged in support of an application for merger?
         (f)   Have full names and addresses been given on page 4?
   (g)   Have you enclosed Inland Revenue form L(A)451 duly completed (if appropriate)?
         (h)   Have you enclosed a certified copy of the constitution of a foreign company?
            Delays may be caused when page 4 is not completed fully and accurately

12   I/We certify that the information required has been supplied and is correct and apply for registration of the
   dealing, in the order or priority shown in panel 2 on page 1.
   A cheque or postal order for £ 160   accompanies this application
   Signature of applicant
   or practitioner   Date 10 July 1990

For official use. Settlers panel (additional).

Page 7

CONVEYANCING

Entry
No.

Edition No.

Opened

A

**6 New proprietors of
the land.**
For single proprietors
enter as follows:—
JOHN SMITH of
29 RYE ROAD,
WATFORD, HERTS
WD3 4TQ, milkman.
For joint proprietors
enter as follows:—
JOHN SMITH, milkman
and MARY SMITH, his
wife, both of 29 RYE
ROAD, WATFORD,
HERTS WD3 4TQ.
If there are no new
proprietors please leave
the white box blank.

B

FREDERICK BROWN AND ADA BROWN
92 BISHOPS STREET

CHARLESTOWN

(Cancel

C

*

**7 New chargee(s)
/mortgagees**
If there is a single new
charge enter as follows
in the white box:—
THE MONEY BANK
PLC of 2 HIGH
STREET, WATFORD,
HERTS, WD2 3PS.
If there are two charges
please enter the first
chargee above the white
box opposite the asterisk
and the second chargee
in the white box.
For BUILDING
SOCIETY charges
only:— please enter the
account number after the
name of the society as
(account no.   ).
If there is no new charge
please leave the white
box blank.

(Date) Charge dated   registered on

to secure | the moneys | therein mentioned
          | the moneys including the further advances |

Proprietor
BIG TOWN BUILDING SOCIETY

1 UPPER ORWELL STREET

TONBRIDGE

registered on

(Cancel   and insert date)

Printed in the United Kingdom for Her Majesty's Stationery Office
Dd 291044 C200 4/89   75p each, 25 for £4.50 or 100 for £16   ISBN 011 390297 2

98

Specimen—abbreviated form

Precedent Conveyance—Seller to Buyer
CONVEYANCE dated   and made between:

(1) THE SELLER: of
(2) THE BUYER: of
WITNESSETH as follows:
IN this Deed 'the Property' means the premises known
as   as the same was more particularly described in
and conveyed by a Conveyance made
the   between
'The purchase price' means the sum of £

The Seller acknowledges receipt from the Buyer of the purchase
price

IN consideration of the purchase price the SELLER
as   HEREBY CONVEYS to the Buyer his freehold
estate in the Property

The Buyer hereby covenants with the Seller by way of indemnity
only to perform and observe the covenants stipulations and other
matters contained or referred to in the said Conveyance mentioned
in Clause 1 hereof and to indemnify the Seller against any liability
resulting from breach or non-observance hereof

The Seller hereby acknowledges the right of the Buyer to production
of the documents listed below and to delivery of copies thereof and
undertakes to keep the originals safe.

Date   *Document*   *Parties*

THE Seller who sells as personal representative of the deceased
named below declares that he has not made any previous
conveyance or transfer of the whole or any part of the property and
hereby acknowledges the right of the Buyer of production of the
Probate of   , deceased which was issued out
of   Probate Registry on
IT IS HEREBY CERTIFIED that this transaction does not form
part of a larger transaction or of a series of transactions in respect
of which the amount or value of the consideration or the aggregate
amount or value of the consideration exceeds £

IN WITNESS whereof the parties have executed this Deed

Specimen—traditional style

THIS ASSIGNMENT is made the
day of   One Thousand Nine Hundred and
BETWEEN   ('the Assignor') of the one part
and   ('the Assignee') of the other part

WHEREAS

(1) The Assignor is seised of the property described in the schedule hereto ('the property') for all the unexpired residue of the term of years granted by the Lease ('the Lease') referred to in Schedule subject to the rent and to the performance observance of the covenants and the conditions contained in the Lease but otherwise free from incumbrances

(2) The Assignor has agreed with the Assignee for the sale of the Property to the Assignee for the unexpired residue of the term of years granted by the Lease

NOW THIS DEED WITNESSETH as follows:

(1) In pursuance of the said agreement and in consideration of the sum of   pounds (£   ) now paid by the Assignee to the Assignor (the receipt whereof the Assignor hereby acknowledges) the Assignor as beneficial owner HEREBY ASSIGNS unto the Assignee ALL AND SINGULAR the property TO HOLD the same unto the Assignee for the unexpired residue of the term of years granted by the Lease SUBJECT henceforth to the payment of the rent and to the performance and observance of the covenants and the conditions contained in the Lease.

(2) IT IS HEREBY CERTIFIED that the transaction hereby effected does not form part of a larger transaction or of a series of transactions in respect of which the amount or value or the aggregate amount or value of the consideration exceeds thirty thousand pounds

IN WITNESS whereof this Assignment has been executed the day and year first before written

The schedule

Lease dated

SIGNED SEALED AND DELIVERED
by the said
in the presence of:

SIGNED SEALED AND DELIVERED
by the said
in the presence of:-

Completion statement

For the sale of
purchase of

Purchase price	£	Proceeds of sale	£
Fees	£	Amount of new mortgage advance	£
Stamp Duty	£		
Land registration fee	£		
Amount required to redeem the subsisting mortgage	£		
Balance due to you	£		
TOTAL	£	TOTAL	£

CHAPTER 9

COMMON PROBLEMS

9.1 Local authority search result

It is important to check the search results received and where there are entries which are not acceptable, the transaction should not continue until adequate explanations have been obtained. Common problems arising from the results of local authority searches include the following:

- An enforcement notice registered against the property. This will indicate that there either is or has been an unauthorised use of the property which was not voluntarily discontinued. It is important to check to what the enforcement notice relates, whether it is now being complied with and whether the authorised use accords with the client buyer's requirement.
- An improvement grant. It is increasingly common for older properties to be renovated with the benefit of an improvement grant from the local authority. Full details of the improvement grant are required because these are registered as a land charge as they carry conditions which affect the property for a period of five years after the date of registration of the grant. Improvement grants are made pursuant to the provisions of the Housing Act 1985 and the relevant conditions must be carefully scrutinised to ensure that the transaction envisaged is authorised and will not result in an obligation to repay the amount of the grant. If such an obligation is imposed, it is important that the seller is required to discharge it.
- Section 52 agreement. Such an agreement was made pursuant to planning permission in respect of the property. It will contain conditions and it is important to obtain a copy of the agreement and confirmation from the seller that the conditions imposed have been fully observed.
- The listing of the buildings. It may be that the property has been listed within a particular category by the Department of the Environment as being of special architectural interest. Such a listing does not necessarily detract from the property but depending upon which category of listing applies it can prevent significant alteration to the overall appearance of the property.
- The property may be situated in a conservation area or smoke control zone under the Clean Air Act 1956. Neither of these

revelations are dramatic but again they affect the freedom of the buyer to enjoy the property.

- The property may not abut a publicly maintained highway. The variable situations which can arise in this regard have previously been discussed and the implication as far as services to the property are concerned should be considered.
- The revelation of planning permission refusals, copies of which have not been sent with replies to preliminary enquiries. The buyer's representative should require the seller's representative to obtain such copies. The last planning permission is important as earlier permissions may have been superseded. Copy refusals are also important because these might be of relevance to the buyer in his future intentions for the property.
- The existence or otherwise of a structure plan by the relevant local government authority and its stage of preparation. Many clients are acutely concerned with their environment and they assume that at the date of buying the property, proposals for development for land in the vicinity will be revealed. This is not necessarily the case and the client buyer should be notified accordingly. If he requires further enquiries to be made, these should be carried out at the local authority as well as asking the seller whether he knows of any proposals for local development.
- Public drainage. The local authority search might reveal the absence of a public drainage system and in such a case the buyer's representative must ascertain whether the property has the benefit of any drainage system and if it is a private drainage system further enquiries should be raised as set out before.

9.2   Preliminary enquiry replies

Many seller's representatives provide guarded replies to preliminary enquiries. Upon receipt of replies to enquiries the form should be read carefully and any enquiries which have been unsatisfactorily answered should be raised again with a view to obtaining a more precise response. Particular matters to be looked for are:

- Boundaries. It is important that the client buyer should acquire what he thinks he is getting and that the seller should have the authority to sell it. Sometimes plans are inaccurate and boundaries have been moved. Sometimes there are ongoing disputes concerning boundaries. The ownership of boundaries may be unclear and boundaries may be dilapidated or even non-existent. The first task of a buyer's representative is to check that the boundaries are precise and accurate and that if they have been moved, this was in agreement with the neighbours, and the deeds accurately reflect the current ownership of the seller. This is particularly important when dealing with the conveyancing of a rural property.

- If the buyer is acquiring a property which is less than ten years old in respect of which there is no NHBC guarantee certificate, a further enquiry should be made as to the status of the builder and whether or not architect's certificates were supplied at the time of construction. Architect's certificates are sufficient to vouch for the good construction of a property and should be obtained by small builders who are not registered with the National House Building Council. If neither exists, the buyer should be advised to have a very thorough survey of the property. This is the only remaining option.

- The seller's representative may draw a distinction between those services which are 'connected' and those services which are 'available'. The difference between the two is obvious but if the buyer client has a gas oven and on completion discovers that the gas main is located some twenty yards away from the property there could be some adverse consequences for the buyer's representative if this fact has not been pointed out to the buyer before contracts are exchanged. It is important to ascertain whether the services cross over neighbouring property and, if so, by what right.

- The authorised use of the property should be established and if this is after 1948 when planning controls commenced, the appropriate planning permissions should be produced. Similarly, if significant alterations have been made to the property within the last few years, any planning permission or building regulations consent should be requested.

- Perhaps the most common area of misunderstanding and dispute when regarding replies to preliminary enquiries is which fixtures and fittings are going to be left and which are going to be removed. With increasing values attaching to all items of property, this question becomes increasingly significant and many firms have adopted the wise practice of preparing a lengthy schedule of all items which may be available and the seller is then required to tick the appropriate column to indicate whether these are included or excluded. Check this list very carefully and report fully to the buyer. If there are areas of disagreement these should be resolved at this stage. Under TransAction there is a specific Fixtures, Fittings and Contents Form.

9.3 Land charge search results

The content of these results has been set out in detail earlier in the text. There are certain entries which do not constitute a problem and which will not be removed such as a D(ii) being a restrictive covenant registered against an earlier owner of the property. There are certain other entries which must be removed on or before completion or at least an undertaking must be obtained from the seller's solicitor to remove it.

Common problems are as follows:

- A puisne mortgage. This is a second or subsequent mortgage which will probably not have been disclosed by the epitome of title and may not be known to the seller's legal representative. This should be cleared off and details must be acquired by the seller as speedily as possible.
- A pending action. The existence of this is not quite so usual but is much more dramatic. If the seller fails to remove this in time for completion, the buyer's representative must not complete. If he does, he will be in breach of his duty to the buyer and the mortgagee, the buyer will not obtain good title and the property would not be readily saleable. A pending action must therefore be removed and if court proceedings against the seller are in existence, they must be hastily concluded with a mutually agreed settlement.
- A writ or order affecting the land. Again, such entries must be removed prior to completion and the seller must make the appropriate payments to the aggrieved persons pursuing him. Once satisfied, those persons must sign a cancellation certificate to secure the cancellation of the entry. That cancellation certificate can then become part of the title deeds.
- An option to purchase. In general, this will relate to a contract to purchase in favour of a third party or an option to purchase in favour of a third party. In either event a C(iv) land charge must be removed by the seller and the buyer must not complete his purchase of the property which remains subject to a C(iv) land charge.

9.4 Replies to requisitions on title

Sometimes the seller's legal representative may be unable to explain apparent defects in the title and in such a case a buyer's representative is entitled to refuse to complete the transaction. Common defects in title have been referred to above.

If there are defects in the title and the buyer nevertheless wishes to continue, such defects must be reported to the proposed mortgagee and its consent to proceeding must be obtained. Most common defects can be solved by obtaining statutory declarations from those with a knowledge of the property supported by a defective title indemnity policy. Such a measure would be regarded as one of last resort and prior to that time efforts may be made to rectify the title by contacting earlier owners. Such matters are carried out at the expense of the seller. Such problems generally do not apply to registered land.

9.5 Dealing with part of land comprised in a title

Dealing with land which only forms part of a title requires separate skills which vary depending on whether the land is registered or unregistered.

The starting point in each case is the obtaining of a good plan which accurately and as precisely as possible defines the boundaries of the parcel of land to be conveyed. This plan should accord with a staked-out area and where possible the boundary measurements should be included.

9.5.1 Unregistered land The procedure is the same as for the sale of the whole except that the conveyance deed will be slightly differently worded. On completion the epitome of title should be returned to the seller's representative with a request that this be 'marked against the original deeds' in his possession. This is an increasingly common practice where the seller's representative has agreed to act as the buyer's agent for the purposes of completion. This task is commonly performed without charge. Where completion takes place in person, the question of examining the epitome against the originals can be dealt with personally by the buyer's representative and he can mark the deeds accordingly for future reference.

A memorandum of this transaction is endorsed on the back of the conveyance to the seller and a certified copy of this is included with the epitome.

The epitome takes the place of the original title deeds and the only original deed handed over on completion is the conveyance to the buyer. This will be placed with any new mortgage deed together with search results relating to the current transaction.

9.5.2 Registered land Conveyancing procedure is the same for registered land for a single title number except that the transfer deed employed is different. It must incorporate a plan and will commonly incorporate new restrictive covenants where the seller retains neigh-bouring property.

The Land Registry search is carried out on Land Registry form 94B and after completion of the purchase the seller's certificate is put on deposit at the Land Registry for the purposes of having a part carved out of it.

The amended certificate is returned to the seller and a new certifi-cate is issued to the buyer on completion of the registration.

CHAPTER 10

FURTHER READING

The most authorative work in this field is *Emmet on Title* (looseleaf, Longman).

Other works which take the material contained in this book further are:

Aldridge, Trevor, *Boundaries, Walls and Fences*, 6th ed (Longman 1986).

Aldridge, Trevor, *Companion to the Standard Conditions of Sale* (Longman, 1990).

Garner, J F, *Rights of Way and Access to the Country side*, 2nd ed (Longman, 1989).

Gregory, Roger, *Stamp Duties for Conveyancers*, 5th ed (Longman, 1990).

O'Hare, John, *Moeran's Practical Conveyancing*, 11th ed (Longman, 1989).

Silverman, Frances, *Standard Conditions of Sale: A Conveyancer's Guide*, 3rd ed (Format Publishing)

Stratton, I G C, *Building Land and Estates: Their Acquisition and Development*, 2nd ed (Longman, 1983).

Timothy, P J, *Wontner's Guide to Land Registry Practice*, 17th ed (Longman, 1989).

Wilkinson, H W, *Pipes, Mains, Cables and Sewers*, 5th ed (Longman, 1989).

Wilkinson, H W, *Standard Conditions of Sale* (Longman 1990).

Law Society and HM Land Registry, *Registered Land Practice Notes*, 2nd ed (Longman, 1986).

Longman Directory of Local Authorities 1990.

For addresses of district land registries and the land charges department, areas served by the district land registries and areas of compulsory registration, see HM Land Registry Explanatory Leaflet No 9, or *Longman Costs and Fees Service* (looseleaf, Longman).

For addresses of local authorities, see *Longman Directory of Local Authorities 1990.*